Java Practice Questions: Oracle Certified Professional, Java SE 7 Programmer (OCPJ)

Esteban Herrera

ISBN-13: 978-1484884744
ISBN-10: 1484884744

Book Website
www.javapracticequestions.com
Email: esteban@javapracticequestions.com

Give feedback on the book at:
esteban@javapracticequestions.com

Printed in U.S.A

Contents

Introduction

Java programmer exams are hard and tricky.

Maybe you have been working with Java for some time. Or you have some projects under your belt. Or you have read some books about the language. Or you know some IDEs (Integrated Development Environment) like Eclipse. However, this kind of experience most of the time is not enough to pass the exam. That is because you must not only be deeply familiar with the features of the language, you also have to understand why some things are the way they are and when and how to use them properly. Like I always say, you must have a java compiler inside your head to pass these exams.

To make things worse, you will be under a lot of time pressure (150 minutes for 90 questions) in an exam with a format that is more about theory (concepts, rules, deciding if a piece of code compiles correctly, etc.) than practice (write a program to do 'X' stuff). Well, at least the questions have multiple answers telling you the number of options to choose.

Moreover, with great efforts come great rewards. I am not going to discuss if getting a certificate is going to help you to make more money or getting a better job faster. A certification may or may not help you achieve those results, but I can assure you that it will give you the knowledge and security to become a best programmer, to take better decisions and be more productive in your daily work.

Starting from Java SE 7, Oracle has broken the programmer certification (the base of all other certifications about Java) in two exams.

The first one, the Oracle Certified Associate Java SE 7 Programmer exam, covers the basics of the language and concepts of object-oriented programming to create simple Java applications. Passing this exam is required to take the second, the Oracle Certified Professional Java SE

7 Programmer exam (the focus of this book) which covers advanced concepts and functionality.

How to use this book

This book should not be your only resource if you are planning to take the second Java SE 7 Programmer exam. It is just intended to be a supplement. A good strategy to pass the exam would be the following:
1. Take a course that covers all the topics of the exam or study with a good study guide.
2. Practice all you can with mock exams.

The purpose behind this book is to help you with the second point. There are many mock exams and simulators offered by companies that claim to have a lot of questions and drills. The problem with most of them is that many of those questions have nothing to do with the topics covered by the exam, are ambiguous, repetitive or simply are just too easy compare it to the real test.

In contrast, this book presents for each of the twelve major topics covered by the exam, 10 well-thought questions properly formatted, each with a reference to its answer and an explanation. You can try to answer the question by yourself and after that see if you got the correct answer before proceeding to the next or answer all the questions within a section, record your answers somewhere and then see how many of them you got right. For all the wrong answers, you can go back to study the topic covered by each question until you master it.

Further, I offer you some tips to pass the exam:
- Write a lot of code, but don't use an IDE (they make your life easier at work, but not for the purpose of study to pass the exam).
- Don't rush through the exam. Do not read the question too quickly, try to fully understand what the question is asking before answer it.
- In questions that involve source code, first of all, check if the code compiles correctly.
- Study one topic at a time.
- Give yourself enough time to study. Avoid cramming.
- Be sure to check out http://www.javaranch.com. It has the best certification forums and a great community.

If you have doubts about the questions presented in this book, you can visit the site http://www.javapracticequestions.com to find information or contact the author.

If you like or find this book helpful, please recommend it. If you don't, please give some feedback to improve it. And let me know how you did in the exam. Good luck.

Esteban Herrera

Practice Questions Section 1. Java Class Design

Objectives:
- Use access modifiers: private, protected, and public
- Override methods
- Overload constructors and other methods appropriately
- Use the instanceof operator and casting
- Use virtual method invocation
- Override methods from the Object class to improve the functionality of your class
- Use package and import statements

1.1. Given:

different package.

```
package p1;
public class A {
  protected int a;

  A() {
    a = 1;
  }

  public void m1() {
    System.out.println(a);
  }
}
package p2;
import p1.A;
public class B {
  public static void main(String[] args) {
    A a1 = new A();
    a1.m1();
  }
}
```

default access Modifier.
Is private - Constructor Private
So B Cannot
create a new
instance.

What is the result when you execute class B?

A. 0

B. 1

C. Compilation fails.

D. An exception is thrown at run time.

View Answer on page 175

1.2. Given:

```
class A {
  public int m1(int i) {
    return i * 2;
  }
}

public class Test extends A {
  public static int m1(int i) {
    return i * 3;
  }

  public static void main(String[] args) {
    Test t = new Test();
    t.m1(1);
  }
}
```

(handwritten annotations: Superclass ← Instance Method; Subclass Static Method override attempt; Should override)

What is the result when you execute class Test?

A. 2

B. 3

C. Compilation fails.

D. An exception is thrown at run time.

View Answer on page 176

1.3. Given:

```java
class A {
  public static void print() {
    print2();
  }

  protected static void print2() {
    System.out.println("A");
  }
}

public class Test extends A {
  public static void print() {
    System.out.println("Test");
  }

  public static void main(String[] args) {
    A instance = new Test();
    instance.print();
  }
}
```

(handwritten annotations: up casting, downcasting, Hides, Subclass, Super class, This is the give away and why printed in A is called not Test)

What is the result when you execute class `Test`?

A. A

B. Test

C. Compilation fails.

D. An exception is thrown at run time.

View Answer on page 177

1.4. Given:

```
class A {
  public int n() {
    return 3;
  }
}

public class Test extends A {
  public int n() {
    return super().n() + 5;
  }
  public static void main(String[] args) {
    A instance = new Test();
    instance.n();
  }
}
```

What is the result when you execute class `Test`?

A. 3

B. 5

C. 8

D. Compilation fails.

E. An exception is thrown at run time.

View Answer on page 178

1.5. Given:

```java
class A {
  public void m1() {
    System.out.println("m1");
  }
}

class B extends A {
  public void m2() {
    System.out.println("m2");
  }
}

class C extends B { }

public class Test {
  public static void main(String[] args) {
    B obj = new B();
    if(obj instanceOf C) {
      obj.m2();
    } else {
      System.out.println("Not an instance");
    }
  }
}
```

What is the result when you execute class Test?

A. m1

B. m2

C. Not an instance

D. Compilation fails.

E. An exception is thrown at run time.

View Answer on page 179

1.6. Given:

```
class A {
  public void m1() {
    System.out.print("Am1 ");
  }
}

public class B extends A {
  public void m1() {
    System.out.print("Bm1 ");
  }

  public void m2() {
    System.out.print("Bm2 ");
  }

  public static void main(String[] args) {
    B objB = new B();
    A objA = (A)objB;
    objA.m1();
    objB.m1();
    objB.m2();
  }
}
```

— overrides M1

Cast

it is still B inside

What is the result when you execute class B?

A. Am1 Bm1 Bm2

B. Bm1 Bm1 Bm2

C. Bm1 Am1 Bm2

D. Compilation fails.

E. An exception is thrown at run time.

View Answer on page 180

1.7. Given:

```java
public class Test {
  public int n = 0;

  public Test(int i) {
    n = i;
  }

  public String toString(Test t) {
    return "[Test: " + t.n + "]";
  }

  public static void main(String[] args) {
    Test obj = new Test(2);
    System.out.println("Hello " + obj);
  }
}
```

call to String() [handwritten annotation]

What is the result when you execute class `Test`?

A. Hello Test

B. Hello [Test: 2]

C. Hello

D. Compilation fails.

E. None of the above.

View Answer on page 181

1.8. Which of the following are valid package declarations? Choose all that apply.

A. org.p1.p2_
B. 123.p1.com *—number first*
C. org.p1._p2
D. org-p1.com *— hyphen*
E. do.p1.com

reserved word

View Answer on page 182

1.9. Given:

```java
class A {
  public void m1() {
    System.out.print("Hello");
  }
}

public class B extends A {
  public static void main(String[] args) {
    A objA = new A();
    B objB = (B)objA;
    objB.m1();
  }
}
```

[handwritten annotation: down Casting objA has no awareness of B will compile but fail at runtime]

What is the result when you execute class B?

A. Nothing is printed.

B. Hello

C. Compilation fails.

D. An exception is thrown at run time.

View Answer on page 183

11

1.10. Which of the following are TRUE statements? Choose all that apply.

A. The `java.lang.Long` class properly override `equals()` and `hashCode()`.

B. There must be one package statement per file, and it applies to all types defined in that file.

C. A method signature includes the return type and the method's name.

D. Casting objects of sibling classes (classes that extend from the same class, but not between them) is considered legal in Java.

E. The `protected` access modifier can be applied to constructors.

View Answer on page 184

class A

Class B extends A

Class C extends A

B test = C new BC);
    is not legal.

Practice Questions Section 1. Java Class Design

Practice Questions Section 2. Advanced Class Design

Objectives:
- Identify when and how to apply abstract classes
- Construct abstract Java classes and subclasses
- Use the static and final keywords
- Create top-level and nested classes
- Use enumerated types

2.1. Given:

```
public abstract class Test {
  abstract void m1(Object o);
}
```

Which of the following declarations are legal?

A. ✗

```
class A extends Test {
  void m1(String o) { }
}
```

Class needs to be abstract or implement M1 properly -

B. ✗

```
class B implements Test {
  void m1(Object o);
}
```

for interfaces not Class. Needs to be extends

C.

✗
```
interface C extends Test {
  void m1(String o);
}
```

Interface cannot extend a Class

D.

✗
```
abstract class D extends Test {
  void m1(String o);
}
```

needs { } or the abstract Modifier

needs imp

E.

✓
```
abstract class D extends Test {
  void m1(String o) { }
}
```

View Answer on page 189

2.2. Which of the following are FALSE statements? Choose all that apply.

A. An abstract class [True] should be used over an interface when some default behavior for the subclasses is needed.
B. One class can implement multiple interfaces. True
C. Interfaces can contain fields that are not static. False
D. A class that implements an interface and provides definitions for all its methods, can still be marked as abstract. True
E. An abstract class cannot have static members. FALSE

View Answer on page 190

2.3. Given:

```
public class Test {
  static Test t;
  static int i = 3;

  public static void main(String[] args) {
    final Test obj;
    obj = new Test(); //1
    Test.t = obj;
    Test.i = 5;
    obj = Test.t; //2
    System.out.println(obj.i);
  }
}
```

What is the result when you execute this program?

A. 3

B. 5

C. Compilation fails at line marked by //1.

D. Compilation fails at line marked by //2.

E. An exception is thrown at run time.

View Answer on page 191

19

2.4. Given:

not initialised

```java
public class Test {
  final static String s;

  Test() {
    s = "hello";
  }

  public static void main(String[] args) {
    Test obj = new Test();
    System.out.println(obj.s);
  }
}
```

class and not instance variable

called on New instance

not intialized

What is the result when you execute this program?

A. hello

B. null

C. Compilation fails.

D. An exception is thrown at run time.

View Answer on page 192

2.5. Given:

```
class A {
  final static void m1() {
    System.out.println("Am1");
  }
}

final public class B extends A {
  static void m1() {
    System.out.println("Bm1");
  }

  public static void main(String[] args) {
    A obj = new B();
    obj.m1();
  }
}
```

Cannot be overridden by subclass (handwritten annotation)

What is the result when you execute class B?

A. Am1

B. Bm1

C. Compilation fails because a final class (B) cannot extend from another class (A).

D. Compilation fails because a final static method cannot be overridden.

E. An exception is thrown at run time.

View Answer on page 193

2.6. Given:

```
public class Test {
  public int i = 5;

  static class A {
    int i = 1; //1
    void m1() {
      System.out.println(i);
    }
  }

  public static void main(String[] args) {
    A obj = new A(); //2
    obj.m1();
  }
}
```

Runs fine because i is declared here

What is the result when you execute class Test?

A. 1

B. 5

C. Compilation fails at line marked by //1.

D. Compilation fails at line marked by //2.

E. An exception is thrown at run time.

View Answer on page 194

2.7. Given:

```
public class Test {
  private int i = 2;

  private class A {
    void m1() {
      i = 3;
      System.out.print(i);
    }
  }

  void m1() {
    new A().m1();
    System.out.print(i);
  }

  public static void main(String[] args) {
    Test obj = new Test();
    obj.m1();
  }
}
```

What is the result when you execute class `Test`?

A. 23

B. 32

C. 33

D. 22

E. Compilation fails.

F. An exception is thrown at run time.

View Answer on page 195

23

2.8. Given:

```
public class Test {
  private class A {
    void m1() {
      m1(1); //1
    }
  }

  void m1(int i) {
    System.out.print(i);
  }

  public static void main(String[] args) {
    Test obj = new Test();
    A a = obj.new A(); //2
    a.m1();
  }
}
```

[handwritten annotations: "Nested Class.", "Method names Cannot be Same in inner & outer", "1", "Correct to create an inner object within the outer object"]

What is the result when you execute class `Test`?

A. 1

B. Compilation fails at line marked by //1.

C. Compilation fails at line marked by //2.

D. An exception is thrown at run time.

E. None of the above.

View Answer on page 196

2.9. Given:

```
public class A {
  static class B {
    void m1() {
      System.out.print("B");
    }
  }
}

public class C {
  class D extends A.B { } //1

  public static void main(String[] args) {
    C obj = new C();
    D a = obj.new D();
    a.m1(); //2
  }
}
```

What is the result when you execute class C? (the above code is all in the same file)

A. B

B. Compilation fails at line marked by //1.

C. Compilation fails at line marked by //2.

D. An exception is thrown at run time.

E. None of the above.

Two public classes cannot exist in same file

View Answer on page 197

2.10. Given:

```
enum MALE {
  MICHAEL(29), PETER(20);

  public MALE(int a) { //1
    this.a = a; //2
  }
  int a;//3
}

public class Test {
  public static void main(String[] args) {
    System.out.println(MALE.MICHAEL.a); //4
  }
}
```

Cannot Invoke a Constructor outside an Enum

What is the result when you execute class `Test`?

A. 29

B. Compilation fails at line marked by //1.

C. Compilation fails at line marked by //2.

D. Compilation fails at line marked by //3.

E. Compilation fails at line marked by //4.

View Answer on page 198

Practice Questions Section 3. Object-Oriented Design Principles

Objectives:
- Write code that declares, implements and/or extends interfaces
- Choose between interface inheritance and class inheritance
- Develop code that implements "is-a" and/or "has-a" relationships
- Apply object composition principles
- Design a class using the Singleton design pattern
- Write code to implement the DAO pattern
- Design and create objects using a factory, and use factories from the API

3.1. Given:

```
public interface A {
  static void m();
}
interface B extends A {
  public int m1();
}
abstract class C implements A, B {
  public int m1() { return 1; }
}
abstract class D extends C implements B {
  public int m1() { return 0; }
}
```

[handwritten notes:] Variables
Implicit public, static e
final.
Methods
Public Abstract
m() Can only be
Masked with
public e
abstract

What is the result when you compile this program?

A. Compilation fails due to an error in interface A.

B. Compilation fails due to an error in interface B.

C. Compilation fails due to an error in class C.

D. Compilation fails due to an error in class D.

E. Compiles successfully.

View Answer on page 203

3.2. Given:

```
interface A {
  public static int i = 3;
  void m();
  void m1();
}

public class Test implements A {
  public void m() {
    System.out.print(i);
  }

  public void m1() {
    System.out.print(i + 3);
  }

  public static void main(String[] args) {
    A obj = new Test();
    obj.m();
    Test.i = 4;
    obj.m1();
  }
}
```

Handwritten annotations: Public Static final A.i — underlined, Cannot reassign

What is the result when you execute class Test?

A. 33

B. 37

C. 36

D. 03

E. 07

F. Compilation fails.

View Answer on page 204

3.3. Which of the following methods from the Java API are examples of the factory pattern? Choose all that apply.

A. `java.lang.Integer#valueOf(int)`
B. `java.util.Calendar#getInstance()`
C. `java.lang.Runtime#getRuntime()`
D. `java.nio.charset.Charset#forName(String charsetName)`
E. `java.util.Arrays#asList(T... a)`

View Answer on page 205

3.4. Given:

```
public class Test {
  static Test t = new Test();
  private Test() { }
  public Test get() { return t; }
}
```

Which of the following statements are true about class `Test`? Choose all that apply.

X **A.** This class represents a Singleton.

✓**B.** This class doesn't represent a Singleton.

X **C.** Compilation fails because an object of a class with a private constructor cannot be created.

X **D.** Compilation fails because a constructor cannot be private.

View Answer on page 206

3.5. Which of the following code fragments implement a valid "has-a" relationship between A and B:

A. ✗
```
public class A extends B {
  void m() {}
}
class B { }
```
"is a" relationship
A "is a" subclass of B

B.
```
class A { }
class B {
  List<A> l;
  void m() {}
}
```
B has a reference to A

C.
```
class A { }
  B b;
}
class B {
  A a;
}
```
A has a reference to B
reverse ditto

D.
```
interface A { }
class B {
  A a;
  void m() {}
}
```
B has a reference to A

E.
```
class A { }
class B { }
```
No relationship

View Answer on page 207

35

3.6. Which of the following code fragments implement a valid "is-a" relationship between A and B:

A.
```
public class A {
  void m() {}
}
class B { }
```
B.
```
class A extends B { }
class B extends A {
  void m() {}
}
```
Circular (cycle not valid in java),
C.
```
interface A {
  void m();
}
class B implements A {
  public void m() {}
}
```
D.
```
class A { }
abstract class B extends A {
  void m() {}
}
```
B is a subclass A
E.
```
class A { }
class B {
  void m(A a) { }
}
```
"has a"

View Answer on page 208

3.7. Which of the following are FALSE statements about the DAO pattern? Choose all that apply.

A. The implementation of the DAO pattern is generally related to the "has-a" relationship.

B. The implementation of the DAO pattern is generally related to the "is-a" relationship.

C. The DAO pattern can be implemented either with an interface or an abstract class. *Abstract factory pattern.*

D. The DAO pattern is directly related to the Transfer Object pattern.

E. DAO stands for Dynamic Access Object.

View Answer on page 209

3.8. Given:

```
class Product {
  public int id;
  public String description;
  public double price;
  public int quantity;
}
abstract class Sale {
  protected int totalItems;
  protected List<Product> products;
  abstract void ship();
  void calculateTotal() {
    // Code to calculate the total of the sale (this is the same
    // for all subclasses)
  }
}
class DigitalSale extends Sale {
  //Digital items are not shipped
  void ship() { }
}
class PhysicalSale extends Sale {
  void ship() {
    //Define behavior to ship physical items
  }
}
```

Single product (handwritten annotation)

Which of the following are TRUE statements? Choose all that apply.

A. Classes Product and DigitalSale participate in a "has-a" relationship.

B. Class Sale should be an interface to reuse code.

C. The shipping behavior could be separated into an interface to make the code more flexible through a "has-a" relationship.

D. It is a good practice to make class DigitalSale abstract and don't provide an empty implementation to ship().

E. It is a good practice to put the calculateTotal() method in the Product class.

Encapsulate what varies (handwritten annotation)
program to interfaces (handwritten annotation)

View Answer on page 210

38

3.9. Which of the following are FALSE statements? Choose all that apply.

A. If we want to provide common functionality to a set of classes is always best to use an abstract class with an "is-a" relationship.

B. A form of multiple inheritance can be achieved through interfaces.

C. You can combine interface inheritance with class inheritance to have the best of both worlds.

D. For designing frameworks, interface inheritance is better than class inheritance because the former provides default implementations.

E. Class inheritance is always implemented in Java with an abstract class.

View Answer on page 211

3.10. Given:

```
class Person {
  public int age;
  public String name;

  public void validateAge() {
    //...
  }

  public void speak() {
    //...
  }

  public void sleep() {
    //...
  }

  public void printValues() {
    //...
  }
}
```

Which of the following are TRUE statements?

A. Class Person uses composition. No "is a" or "has a" relationship

B. Class Person uses inheritance. No

C. Class Person has a high cohesion. No does too much

✓ **D.** Class Person has a low cohesion. Yes as above.

E. Class Person is encapsulated. everything is public so no

✓ **F.** Class Person is not encapsulated. every is public

View Answer on page 212

Practice Questions Section 4. Generics and Collections

Objectives:
- Create a generic class
- Use the diamond syntax to create a collection
- Analyze the interoperability of collections that use raw type and generic types
- Use wrapper classes and autoboxing
- Create and use a List, a Set and a Deque
- Create and use a Map
- Use java.util.Comparator and java.lang.Comparable
- Sort and search arrays and lists

4.1. Given:

```
class A<X, Y extends X> {
  private X t;
  public void set(Y t) { this.t = t; }
  public X get() { return t; }
}
class B { }
class C extends B { }
class D { }
```

Which of the following are valid uses of class A?

A. `class E extends A<C, B> {}`

B. `A a = new A();`

C. `A<D, D> a = new A();`

D. `A<X, Y> a = new A<X, Y> ();`

E. `A a = new A<Object, A<B, C>>();`

View Answer on page 217

45

4.2. Given:

```
public class Test {
  public void m(List<Integer> l) {
    System.out.print(l.size());
  }

  public void m1() {
    List<Integer> l = new ArrayList<>(); //1
    l.add(1);
    l.add(2);
    m(l);
    m(new ArrayList<>()); //2
  }
  public static void main(String[] args) {
    Test obj = new Test();
    obj.m1();
  }
}
```

[handwritten annotations: Compiler See's — new ArrayList<object>() — needs ArrayList<integer>() ; Type inference limited]

What is the result when you execute class Test? (Assuming the correct imports)

A. Compilation fails at line marked by //1

B. Compilation fails at line marked by //2

C. 20

D. None of the above.

View Answer on page 218

4.3. Given:

```
public class Test {

    public static void main(String[] args) {
        List<Integer> l1 = new ArrayList<>();
        l1.add(1);
        List l2 = l1;
        l2.add("hello");
        List<Integer> l3 = l2;
        l3.add(2);
        System.out.println(l1);
    }
}
```

Parametensed type

Raw type L2 = L1 allowed

warning

adding raw to parametrized

What is the result when you execute class Test? (Assuming the correct imports)

A. [1, 2]

B. [1]

C. [1, hello, 2]

D. Compilation fails.

E. An exception is thrown at run time.

View Answer on page 219

47

4.4. Given:

```
public class Test {
  public static void main(String[] args) {
    List<Long> ll = new ArrayList<>();
    ll.add(1);
    ll.add(new Long(2));
    ll.add(Long.parseLong("3"));
    System.out.println(ll.get(0));
  }
}
```

[handwritten: converts primitive type to Int but has to be long: Compiler ERROR]

What is the result when you execute class Test? (Assuming the correct imports)

A. 1

B. 2

C. 3

D. Compilation fails.

E. An exception is thrown at run time.

View Answer on page 220

4.5. Given:

```
public class Test {
  public static void main(String[] args) {
    List <Integer> l1 = new ArrayList<>();
    l1.add(30);
    l1.add(23);
    l1.add(1,0);
    List <Integer> l2 = new ArrayList<>(l1);
    l2.addAll(l1);
    l2.add(4,9);
    List <Integer> l3 = l2.subList(2, 5);
    l3.clear();
    System.out.println(l2);
  }
}
```

What is the result when you execute class Test? (Assuming the correct imports)

A. [30, 1, 23, 30, 4, 1, 23]

B. [30, 1, 1, 23]

C. [30, 0, 23]

D. [30, 0, 0, 23]

E. An exception is thrown at run time.

F. None of the above.

View Answer on page 221

4.6. Given:

```
public class Test {
   public static void main(String[] args) {
      Set<Integer> s1 = new HashSet<>();
      s1.add(30);
      s1.add(23);
      s1.add(null);
      Set<Integer> s2 = new HashSet<>(s1);
      s2.addAll(s1);
      System.out.println(s2.size());
   }
}
```

What is the result when you execute class Test? (Assuming the correct imports)

A. 2

B. 3

C. 6

D. 9

E. None of the above

View Answer on page 222

4.7. Given:

```
public class Test {
  public static void main(String[] args) {
    Queue<Integer> q = new PriorityQueue<>();
    for (int i = 0; i <= 5; i++)
      q.add(i);
    q.peek();q.poll();q.peek();q.poll();
    System.out.println(q);
  }
}
```

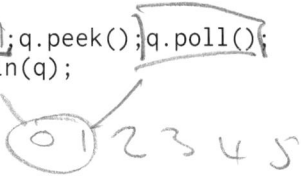

What is the result when you execute class `Test`? (Assuming the correct imports)

A. [2, 3]
B. [3, 2]
C. [5, 4, 3, 2]
D. [2, 3, 4, 5]
E. None of the above.

View Answer on page 223

4.8. Which of the following are FALSE statements? Choose all that apply.

A. All keys in a map must be unique.

B. The `Map` interface extends the `Collection` interface.

C. Maps don't support iterators.

D. The `Map` interface only has two implementations, `HashMap` and `TreeMap`.

E. It is possible to change the value associated with a key with the method `setValue` of the interface `Map.Entry` while iterating the `Map`.

View Answer on page 224

[Handwritten notes:]

- Identify HashMap
- linked Hash map
- weak hashmap

Tree Map

19 different HashMaps

4.9. Given:

```
class A implements Comparator<A> {
  private String s1;
  A(String s1) {
    this.s1 = s1;
  }

  public int compare(A o1, A o2) {
    return o1.s1.compareTo(o2.s1);
  }

  public String toString() {
    return s1;
  }
}

public class Test {

  public static void main(String[] args) {
    List<A> l = new ArrayList<>();
    l.add(new A("a1"));
    l.add(new A("m2"));
    l.add(new A("b5"));
    Collections.sort(l);
    System.out.println(l);
  }
}
```

What is the result when you execute class Test? (Assuming the correct imports)

A. [a1, b5, m2]

B. [m2, b5, a1]

C. [a1, m2, b5]

D. Compilation fails.

E. An exception is thrown at run time.

View Answer on page 225

4.10. Which of the following are TRUE statements? Choose all that apply.

X **A.** SortedMap implementations have a constructor that takes a Comparable. *Spelling Comparator*

✓ **B.** java.util.Date implements the Comparable interface.

X **C.** A SortedMap maintains its entries in descending order, according to the keys' natural ordering, if an implementation of Comparator is not provided. *Ascending*

✓ **D.** TreeSet has a comparator method that returns the Comparator used (if any).

✓ **E.** Collections.binarySearch has a version that takes a List and an element to search for. It assumes that the List is sorted in ascending order according to the natural ordering of its elements.

View Answer on page 226

Practice Questions Section 5.
String Processing

Objectives:
- Search, parse and build strings
- Search, parse, and replace strings by using regular expressions, using expression patterns for matching limited to: . (dot), * (star), + (plus), ?, \d, \D, \s, \S, \w, \W, \b. \B, [], ().
- Format strings using the formatting parameters: %b, %c, %d, %f, and %s in format strings.

5.1. Given:

```
public class Test {
  public static void main(String[] args) {
    String s = "hello";
    s.concat(" ");
    char[] arr = { 'w', 'o', 'r', 'l', 'd' };
    String s2 = new String(arr);
    s.concat(s2);
    if(s == "hello") {
      System.out.println(s);
    } else {
      System.out.println(s2);
    }
  }
}
```

What is the result when you execute this program?

A. hello

B. hello world

C. world

D. None of the above.

E. Compilation fails.

View Answer on page 231

5.2. Given:

```
public class Test {
  public static void main(String[] args) {
    String s = String.format("%d, %s, %b",
        5,
        2.12,
        0);
    System.out.println(s);
  }
}
```

What is the result when you execute this program?

A. 5, , false

B. 5, 2.12, false

C. 5, 2.12, true

D. Compilation fails.

E. An exception is thrown at run time.

View Answer on page 232

5.3. Which of the following are valid format strings for a floating point number? Choose all that apply.

A. `%-99.5f`.
B. `%2f`.
C. `%2$.5f`.
D. `%f5`.
E. `%-.2f`.

View Answer on page 233

5.4. Which of the following are TRUE statements? Choose all that apply.

A. Wrapper classes (`Byte`, `Integer`, `Double`, `Float`, `Long`, `Boolean`, and `Short`) each provide a static method named `valueOf` that converts an object of that type to a string.

B. One way to convert a number to a string is with `String.valueOf(i)` where i represents an `int`.

C. All wrapper classes include a static `toString` method, that converts the primitive type to a string.

D. `java.lang.Integer` provides methods of type `parseXXX()` for all primitive types (for example, `parseBoolean()` and `parseDouble()`) that can be used to convert a string to primitive types.

E. An easy way to convert a `char` to `String` is to concatenate the `char` value to an empty string.

View Answer on page 234

5.5. Given:

```
public class Test {
  public static void main(String[] args) {
    String s = "55 aaa 77 bbb 88 ccc";
    String[] arr = s.split("\\d\\s");
    for(String a : arr) System.out.println(a);
  }
}
```

What is the result when you execute this program?

A.

55

aaa

77

bbb

88

ccc

B.

5

aaa 7

bbb 8

ccc

C.

5 aaa

7 bbb

8 ccc

D.

5

7

8

E. Compilation fails.

F. An exception is thrown at run time.

View Answer on page 235

5.6. Given:

```
public class Test {
  public static void main(String[] args) {
    Pattern p = Pattern.compile("Hello Hello hello world");
    Matcher m = p.matcher("hello");
    if(m.matches())
      System.out.println(1);
    else
      System.out.println(2);
  }
}
```

What is the result when you execute this program? (Assuming the correct imports)

A. 1

B. 2

C. Compilation fails.

D. An exception is thrown at run time.

View Answer on page 236

5.7. Given:

```
public class Test {
  public static void main(String[] args) {
    Pattern p = Pattern.compile("\\d?");
    Matcher m = p.matcher("ac56j85");
    while(m.find())
      System.out.println(m.start() + ", " + m.group());
  }
}
```

What is the result when you execute this program? (Assuming the correct imports)

A.

2, 56

5, 85

B.

5, 2

6, 3

8, 5

5, 6

C.

2, 5

3, 6

5, 8

6, 5

7,

D.

2, 5

3, 6

5, 8

6, 5

E.

1,

2, 56

3,

4,

5, 85

6,

7,

F. None of the above.

View Answer on page 237

5.8. Given:

```
public class Test {
  public static void main(String[] args) {
    Pattern p = Pattern.compile("\\\\");
    String s = "abc\\d\\\\efg";
    System.out.println(p.matcher(s).replaceFirst("11"));
  }
}
```

What is the result when you execute this program? (Assuming the correct imports)

A. abc\d\\efg

B. abc\d11efg

C. abc11d\\efg

D. abc\d11\efg

E. Compilation fails.

View Answer on page 238

5.9. Given:

```java
public class Test {
  public static void main(String[] args) {
    String str = "1 + 2 + 1 + 3 + 1 + 4";
    int i = str.indexOf("1");
    while(i >= 0) {
      System.out.print(i + " ");
      i = str.indexOf('1', i+1);
    }
  }
}
```

What is the result when you execute this program?

A. 1 9 17

B. 8 16

C. 9 17

D. 0 8 16

E. Compilation fails.

F. An exception is thrown at run time.

View Answer on page 239

5.10. Which of the following are FALSE statements? Choose all that apply.

A. In a regular expression, you can specify sets of characters to search for using parenthesis.

B. \s matches whitespace and the underscore characters.

C. The method `substring(int beginIndex, int endIndex)` returns a string that is a substring of the string in which is invoked. The second argument is the index of the last character minus one.

D. An invocation of the method `String.split(regex, n)` yields the same result as the method `Pattern.compile(regex).split(String, n)`.

E. The `Pattern` class can accept a set of flags affecting the way the pattern is matched.

View Answer on page 240

Practice Questions Section 6. Exceptions and Assertions

Objectives:
- Use throw and throws statements
- Use the try statement with multi-catch, and finally clauses
- Autoclose resources with a try-with-resources statement
- Create custom exceptions
- Test invariants by using assertions

6.1. Given:

```
public class Test {
  public static int i = 1;
  public static void main(String[] args) {
    if(i % 0 == 1) {
      throw IllegalStateException;
    }
    System.out.println(i);
  }
}
```

What is the result when you execute this program?

A. 1

B. An exception of type `java.lang.IllegalStateException` is thrown at run time.

C. Compilation fails.

D. None of the above.

View Answer on page 245

6.2. Given:

```
public class Test {
  public static void main(String[] args) {
    try {
      m();
      System.out.print("1");
    } catch(Exception e) {
      System.out.print("2");
    }
  }

  public static void m() {
    m1();
  }

  public static void m1() throws Exception {
    throw new Exception();
  }
}
```

What is the result when you execute this program?

A. 1

B. 12

C. 2

D. Compilation fails.

E. An exception is thrown at run time.

View Answer on page 246

6.3. Given:

```
public class A extends Exception {}

class B extends A {}

class C {
 public void m() throws A { }
}

class D extends C {
 public void m() throws B { }
}

class E extends D {
 public void m() throws A { }
}
```

What is the result when you compile this program?
A.Compilation fails at class A.
B. Compilation fails at class B.
C. Compilation fails at class C.
D. Compilation fails at class D.
E. Compilation fails at class E.
F. None of the above.

View Answer on page 247

6.4. Given:

```
public class Test {
  public static int i = 1;
  public static void main(String[] args) {
    for (int i = 0; i < 5; i++) {
      assert i % 2 == 1 : m();
      System.out.print(i);
    }
  }

  public static String m() {
    return "error";
  }
}
```

What is the result when you execute this program? Choose all that apply.

A. It prints "0" followed by an `AssertionError` (without a message) if assertions are enabled at runtime.

B. It prints "0" followed by an `AssertionError` with the message error if assertions are enabled at runtime.

C. An `AssertionError` with the message "error" will be thrown if assertions are enabled at runtime.

D. Compilation fails if assertions are not enabled at runtime.

E. It prints "01234" if assertions are not enabled at runtime.

F. It prints "13" if assertions are not enabled at runtime.

View Answer on page 248

6.5. Given:

```
public class Test {
  public static void main(String[] args) {
    System.out.println(m());
  }

  public static String m() {
    try {
      assert false;
    } catch (AssertionError e) { //1
      return "error";
    }
    return "success"; //2
  }
}
```

What is the result when you execute this program with assertions disabled?

A. error

B. success

C. Compilation fails at line marked by //1.

D. Compilation fails at line marked by //2.

E. None of the above.

View Answer on page 249

6.6. Which of the following are TRUE statements? Choose all that apply.

A. The try-with-resources statement can declare more than one resource that must be closed.

B. Only objects which implement `java.io.Closeable` can be used as resources in a try-with-resources statement.

C. A try-with-resources statement cannot have a `finally` block.

D. The `close` method of the resources declared in a try-with-resources statement are called in the same order of the resources declaration.

E. In a try-with-resources statement, its `catch` blocks are executed after the resources declared have been closed.

View Answer on page 250

6.7. Given:

```
class R implements AutoCloseable {
  public void close() throws Exception {
    throw new Exception("Close");
  }

  public void read() throws Exception {
    throw new Exception("Read");
  }
}
public class Test {
  public static void main(String[] args) {
    try(R r = new R()) {
      r.read();
    } catch (Exception e) {
      System.out.println(e.getMessage());
    }
  }
}
```

What is the result when you execute class Test?

A.

Read

Close

B.

Close

Read

C.

Close

D.

Read

E. Compilation fails.

View Answer on page 251

6.8. Given:

```
public class Test {
  public static void main(String[] args) {
    try {
      Class.forName("class").newInstance();
    } catch (IllegalAccessException e | InstantiationException i
              | ClassNotFoundException f) {
      if(e != null) {
        System.out.println("e");
      }
      else if(i != null) {
        System.out.println("i");
      }
      else if(f != null) {
        System.out.println("f");
      }
    }
  }
}
```

What is the result when you execute this program?

A. e

B. i

C. f

D. Compilation fails.

E. An exception is thrown at run time.

View Answer on page 252

6.9. Given:

```
class A extends RuntimeException {}
 public class Test extends Exception {
   public static void main(String[] args) throws A, Test {
     try {
       if ("" == "") {
         throw new A();
       } else {
         throw new Test();
       }
     } catch(Exception e) {
       throw e;
     }
   }
 }
}
```

What is the result when you execute class Test?

A. An exception of type A is thrown at run time.

B. An exception of type Test is thrown at run time.

C. An exception of type Exception is thrown at run time.

D. Compilation fails.

View Answer on page 253

6.10. Given:

```
public class Test {
  public static void main(String[] args) {
    try {
      Object i = new Long(0);
      int total = 100/(Integer)i;
      System.out.println(total);

    } catch(ArithmeticException | IllegalArgumentException e) {

      e = new RuntimeException("Test");

      throw e;

    }

  }
}
```

What is the result when you execute this program?

A. An exception with the message "Test" is printed.

B. 0

C. Compilation fails.

D. An uncaught exception is thrown at run time.

View Answer on page 254

Practice Questions Section 7. Java I/O Fundamentals

Objectives:
- Read and write data from the console
- Use streams to read and write files

7.1. Given:

```
public class Test {
  public static void main(String[] args) throws IOException {
    try (FileInputStream in = new FileInputStream("in.txt");
       FileOutputStream out = new FileOutputStream("out.txt")) {
      byte b = 0;
      while ((b = in.read()) != -1) {
        out.write(b);
      }
    }
  }
}
```

What is the result when you execute this program? (Assuming the correct imports and that in.txt exists and is not an empty file)

A. An empty file out.txt

B. File out.txt with the same content than in.txt

C. Compilation fails.

D. An uncaught exception is thrown at run time.

View Answer on page 259

7.2. Which of the following are FALSE statements? Choose all that apply.

A. Classes `java.io.FileReader` and `java.io.FileWriter` are byte-oriented.

B. `PrintWriter.println` uses the same line terminator that is used in the input file when copying from one file to another.

C. `System.in` is a character stream.

D. Java provides three standard streams: `System.in`, `System.out`, and `System.err`.

E. Buffered streams call native APIs only when the buffer is full (output) or empty (input).

View Answer on page 260

7.3. Given:

```
public class Test {
  public static void main(String[] args) throws IOException {
    try (PrintWriter pw = new PrintWriter("out.txt")) {
      pw.printf("%s", "pw");
    }

    try (FileWriter fw = new FileWriter("out.txt")) {
      fw.printf("%s", "fw");
    }
  }
}
```

What is the result when you execute this program? (Assuming the correct imports and that out.txt doesn't exists)

A. File out.txt with the content:

pw

fw

B. File out.txt with the content:

fw

C. Compilation fails.

D. An uncaught exception is thrown at run time.

View Answer on page 261

7.4. Which of the following are TRUE statements about `System.console()`? Choose all that apply.

A. Its method `readLine()` supports secure password entry, making the password invisible on the user's screen.
B. `System.console` can return `null` if console operations are not permitted, either because the OS doesn't support them or because the program was launched in a non-interactive environment.
C. The `Console` object provides input and output streams that are true character streams, through its `reader` and `writer` methods.
D. `System.out` uses the default platform encoding, while the output methods of the `Console` class use the console encoding.

View Answer on page 262

7.5. Given:

```
public class Test {
  public static void main(String[] args) throws IOException {
    Path p = FileSystems.getDefault().getPath("c:\\1.txt");

    try (OutputStream out
        = new BufferedOutputStream(Files.newOutputStream(p))) {
      String s = "hello";
      byte data[] = s.getBytes();
      out.write(data, 0, data.length);
    }

    try (OutputStream out
        = new BufferedOutputStream(Files.newOutputStream(p))) {
      String s = "world";
      byte data[] = s.getBytes();
      out.write(data, 0, data.length);
    }
  }
}
```

What is the result when you execute this program? (Assuming the correct imports and that "c:\1.txt" doesn't exists)

A. File c:\1.txt with the content:

world

B. File c:\1.txt with the content:

hello

world

C. File c:\1.txt with the content:

helloworld

D. Compilation fails.

E. An uncaught exception is thrown at run time.

View Answer on page 263

7.6. Which of the following are valid ways to read a file? Choose all that apply.

A.
```
Path p = ...;
byte[] fileArray = Files.readAllCharacters(p);
```
B.
```
Path p = ...;
try (BufferedReader r = Files.newBufferedReader(p, Charset.
forName("UTF-8"))) {
  String l = null;
  while ((l = r.readLine()) != null) {
    //...
  }
} catch (IOException x) {
    //...
}
```
C.
```
try (BufferedReader reader = new BufferedReader(new
InputStreamReader(System.in))) {
  String l = null;
  while ((l = r.readLine()) != null) {
    //...
  }
} catch (IOException x) {
    //...
}
```
D.
```
Path p = ...;
byte[] fileArray = Files.readAllBytes(p);
```

View Answer on page 264

7.7. Given:

```
public class Test {
  public static void main(String[] args) {
    Path p = FileSystems.getDefault().getPath("c:\\1.txt");
    try {
      Files.createFile(p);
    } catch (IOException x) {
      System.out.println("Error");
    }
  }
}
```

What is the result when you execute this program? (Assuming the correct imports and that "c:\1.txt" exists and has the line "hello" as content)

A. The file is replaced with a new and empty file.

B. Since the file already exists, the program leaves it as it is.

C. "Error" is printed.

D. Compilation fails.

E. An uncaught exception is thrown at run time.

View Answer on page 265

7.8. Given:

```
public class Test {
  public static void main(String[] args) throws IOException {
    Path p = FileSystems.getDefault().getPath("c:\\1.txt");
    int c = 0;
    try (SeekableByteChannel sbc = Files.newByteChannel(p)) {
      ByteBuffer b = ByteBuffer.allocate(10); //1
      while ((c = sbc.read(b)) > 0) {
        b.rewind(); //2
        for(int i = 0; i < c; i++)
          System.out.print((char)b.get()); //3
      }
    }
  }
}
```

Which of the following are TRUE statements about this program? (Assuming the correct imports and that "c:\1.txt" exists and has the line "hello" as content)

A. The throws clause of method main is optional. Nothing in this code could throw an IOException.

B. Since the file already exists, the program truncates it and nothing is printed.

C. The line marked by //1 allocates a buffer of 10 bytes.

D. The line marked by //2 is required to print the content of the buffer.

E. The line marked by //3 reads the byte at the buffer's current position, and then, increments that position.

View Answer on page 266

7.9. Given:

```
public class Test {
  public static void main(String[] args) throws IOException {
    try (OutputStream os = new FileOutputStream("c:\\1.txt")) {
      BufferedOutputStream bos = new BufferedOutputStream(os);
      DataOutputStream dos = new DataOutputStream(bos);
      String s = "hello world";
      byte[] b = s.getBytes();
      dos.write(b);
    }
  }
}
```

What is the result when you execute this program? (Assuming the correct imports and that "c:\1.txt" doesn't exist)

A. An empty file is generated.

B. A file with the content "hello world" is generated.

C. No file is generated.

D. Compilation fails.

E. An uncaught exception is thrown at run time.

View Answer on page 267

7.10. Given:

```
public class Test {
  public static void main(String[] args) throws IOException {
    Console c = System.console();
    char [] passw = c.readPassword("Enter your old password: ");
    Arrays.fill(passw, ' ');
    System.out.println(passw);
  }
}
```

Which of the following are FALSE statements about this program?
Choose all that apply. (Assuming the correct imports)

A. The program will present the string `"Enter your old password: "`
as prompt text.

B. A `java.io.IOException` is never thrown by this code.

C. Compilation fails.

D. An uncaught exception is thrown at run time when the program is
run from an IDE like Eclipse.

View Answer on page 268

Practice Questions Section 8. Java File I/O (NIO.2)

Objectives:
- Use the Path class to operate on file and directory paths
- Use the Files class to check, delete, copy, or move a file or directory
- Read and change file and directory attributes
- Recursively access a directory tree
- Find a file by using the PathMatcher class
- Watch a directory for changes by using WatchService

8.1. Given:

```
public class Test {
  public static void main(String[] args) {
    Path path = Paths.get("C:\\temp\\a\\b\\c\\1.txt");
    System.out.print(path.getName(1) + " ");
    System.out.print(path.getNameCount() + " ");
    System.out.print(path.subpath(1,3));
  }
}
```

What is the result when you execute this program in Windows?
(Assuming the correct imports)

A. temp 6 temp\a\b

B. temp 6 temp\a\b\c

C. temp 5 temp\a\b

D. a 5 a\b

E. An uncaught exception is thrown at run time.

View Answer on page 273

8.2. Given:

```java
public class Test {
  public static void main(String[] args) {
    Path p1 = Paths.get("C:\\temp\\a\\b\\c\\1.txt");
    Path p2 = Paths.get("C:\\a\\..\\temp\\a\\b\\c\\1.txt");
    Path p3 = Paths.get("C:\\temp\\A\\b\\c\\1.txt");

    if(p1.equals(p2)) {
      System.out.print(1);
    }

    if(p1.compareTo(p2) == 0) {
      System.out.print(2);
    }
    if(p1.equals(p3)) {
      System.out.print(3);
    }
  }
}
```

What is the result when you execute this program in Windows?
(Assuming the correct imports)

A. 123

B. 12

C. 1

D. 23

E. 3

View Answer on page 274

8.3. Given:

```
public class Test {
  public static void main(String[] args) throws IOException {
    Path p = Paths.get("C:\\temp\\a\\b\\c\\1.txt");

    if(Files.exists(p)) {
      System.out.print(1);
    }
    if(Files.notExists(p)) {
      System.out.print(2);
    }
    if(Files.isReadable(p)) {
      System.out.print(3);
    }
    if(Files.isExecutable(p)) {
      System.out.print(4);
    }
  }
}
```

Which of the following are TRUE statements about this program? Choose all that apply. (Assuming the correct imports)

A. Compilation fails.

B. If the file doesn't exist nothing will be printed.

C. If the file doesn't exist an exception will be thrown.

D. If the existence of the file cannot be determined, `Files.exists(p)` and `Files.notExists(p)` will yield the same result.

E. If the Java Virtual Machine has insufficient privileges to read the file an exception will be thrown.

View Answer on page 275

8.4. Given:

```
public class Test {
  public static void main(String[] args) throws IOException {
    Path p = Paths.get("C:\\temp\\a\\b\\c\\1");
    Files.delete(p);
  }
}
```

Which of the following are FALSE statements about this program?
Choose all that apply. (Assuming the correct imports)
A. Compilation fails.
B. If the path object represents a non-empty directory, an exception
will be thrown.
C. If the path object represents a file that doesn't exist the method will
fail silently (no exception will be thrown).
D. If the path object represents an existing file, this program will
always delete it, even if it is being used by another process.
E. If the path object represents a directory and you are not sure if
the directory exists, you can use the method deleteIfExists(Path)
instead if you don't want an exception to be thrown.

View Answer on page 276

8.5. Which of the following are valid ways to copy a symbolic link (not the target, but the link itself)? Choose all that apply.

A. `Files.copy(source, target);`
B. `Files.copy(source, target, StandardCopyOption.COPY_`
`ATTRIBUTES);`
C. `Files.copy(source, target, StandardCopyOption.REPLACE_`
`EXISTING);`
D. `Files.copy(source, target, LinkOption.NOFOLLOW_LINKS);`
E. It cannot be done.

View Answer on page 277

8.6. Given:

```
public class Test {
 public static void main(String[] args) {
   Path p = Paths.get("C:\\");
   Path f = p.resolve("1.txt");

   try {
     BasicFileAttributes basicFileAttributes = Files.
           readAttributes(f, BasicFileAttributes.class);
     System.out.println("isDirectory: " +
           basicFileAttributes.isDirectory());
    System.out.println("size: " + basicFileAttributes.size());
     System.out.println("isRegularFile: " +
           basicFileAttributes.isRegularFile());
     System.out.println("creationTime: " +
           basicFileAttributes.creationTime());
     System.out.println("lastAccessTime: " +
           basicFileAttributes.lastAccessTime());
     System.out.println("lastModifiedTime: " +
           basicFileAttributes.lastModifiedTime());

     DosFileAttributes dosFileAttributes = Files.
           readAttributes(f, DosFileAttributes.class);
     System.out.println("isHidden: " +
           dosFileAttributes.isHidden());
     System.out.println("isReadOnly: " +
           dosFileAttributes.isReadOnly());
     System.out.println("isSystem: " +
           dosFileAttributes.isSystem());
     System.out.println("isArchive: " +
           dosFileAttributes.isArchive());

     PosixFileAttributes posixFileAttributes = Files.
           readAttributes(f, PosixFileAttributes.class); //1
     System.out.println("owner: " +
           posixFileAttributes.owner().getName());
     System.out.println("group: " +
           posixFileAttributes.group().getName());
    System.out.println("permissions: " + PosixFilePermissions.
           toString(posixFileAttributes.permissions()));

     //Files.setHidden(f, true); //2
   } catch(IOException ex) {
     System.out.println("Error");
   }
```

```
    }
}
```

Which of the following are TRUE statements about this program? Choose all that apply. (Assuming the correct imports)

A. Compilation fails.

B. If the file doesn't exist, `"Error"` will be printed.

C. If the file doesn't exist, an uncaught exception will be thrown.

D. If the file exists and this program is run on Windows, a runtime exception will be thrown at line marked by //1.

E. If the line marked by //2 is uncommented, the program won't compile.

View Answer on page 279

8.7. Given:

```java
class A implements FileVisitor<Path> {
  public FileVisitResult preVisitDirectory(Path dir,
      BasicFileAttributes attrs) throws IOException {
    System.out.println("preVisitDirectory: " + dir.toString());
    return FileVisitResult.CONTINUE;
  }
  public FileVisitResult visitFile(Path file,
      BasicFileAttributes attrs) throws IOException {
    System.out.println(file.toString());
    return FileVisitResult.CONTINUE;
  }
  public FileVisitResult visitFileFailed(Path file,
      IOException exc) throws IOException {
    System.out.println("visitFileFailed: " + file.toString());
    return FileVisitResult.CONTINUE;
  }
  public FileVisitResult postVisitDirectory(Path dir,
      IOException exc) throws IOException {
    System.out.println("postVisitDirectory: " + dir.toString());
    return FileVisitResult.CONTINUE;
  }
}

public class Test {
  public static void main(String[] args) throws IOException {
    Path p = Paths.get("C:\\temp");
    Files.walkFileTree(p, new A());
  }
}
```

Which of the following are TRUE statements about this program?
Choose all that apply. (Assuming the correct imports)

A. If `"C:\\temp"` represents a non-existing directory, the program will throw a `java.io.IOException`.

B. If `"C:\\temp"` represents a file, methods `preVisitDirectory` and `postVisitDirectory` won't be executed.

C. If `"C:\\temp"` represents an existing directory, the program will visit all of its subdirectories recursively.

D. The program doesn't compile. `java.nio.file.FileVisitor` is not an interface.

E. The method `Files.walkFileTree` takes as a second argument, a `FileVisitor` instance only with a type argument that is an instance or a subclass of `java.nio.file.Path`.

View Answer on page 280

8.8. Which of the following are FALSE statements? Choose all that apply.

A. If the `FileVisitor.preVisitDirectory` method returns `FileVisitResult.CONTINUE`, the current directory will be visited.
B. If the `FileVisitor.preVisitDirectory` method returns `FileVisitResult.TERMINATE`, the current directory will be skipped.
C. If the `FileVisitor.postVisitDirectory` method returns `FileVisitResult.SKIP_SIBLINGS`, no further sibling directories will be visited.
D. If the `FileVisitor.preVisitDirectory` method returns `FileVisitResult.SKIP_SUBTREE`, the subdirectories of the current directory will be skipped, but the files of the current directory will be visited.
E. If the `FileVisitor.visitFile` method returns `FileVisitResult.SKIP_NEXT_FILE`, the next file to be visited is skipped.

View Answer on page 281

8.9. Given:

```
PathMatcher matcher =
                FileSystems.getDefault().
                    getPathMatcher("glob:[!f.]?{z[A-E]}");
//1
if (matcher.matches(p)) {
  System.out.println(1);
}
```

Which of the following declarations of p can be inserted at the line marked by //1 to make the program print 1?

A. `Path p = Paths.get("!hzA");`

B. `Path p = Paths.get(",9zE");`

C. `Path p = Paths.get("f.zC");`

D. `Path p = Paths.get("a1zF");`

E. `Path p = Paths.get("kzB");`

View Answer on page 282

8.10. Which of the following are TRUE statements about using the class WatchService? Choose all that apply.

A. The watch service exits when either the thread exits or when the service is closed (by invoking its close() method).

B. Since the Path class doesn't implement the interface Watchable, you have to subclass it to implement that interface and register it with the watch service.

C. java.nio.file.StandardWatchEventKinds only supports the types of events modify and delete.

D. A watch key can have the Invalid state that indicates that the key is no longer active, when for example, the watched directory becomes inaccessible.

E. Once a watch key acquires the Signaled state, it is no longer in the Ready state until its reset method is invoked and it cannot receive any further events.

View Answer on page 283

Practice Questions Section 9. Building Database Applications with JDBC

Objectives:
- Define the layout of the JDBC API
- Connect to a database by using a JDBC driver
- Update and query a database
- Customize the transaction behavior of JDBC and commit transactions
- Use the JDBC 4.1 RowSetProvider, RowSetFactory, and RowSet interfaces

9.1. Which are the correct steps when using JDBC to process a query?

A. Create a Statement object, establish a connection, execute the query, process the ResultSet object, and close the connection.
B. Establish a connection, create a Statement object, execute the query, process the ResultSet object, and close the connection.
C. Establish a connection, execute the query, process the ResultSet object, and close the connection.
D. Establish a connection, execute the query, and close the connection.

View Answer on page 287

9.2. Given:

```
public class Test {
  public static void main(String[] args) {
    Properties props = new Properties();
    props.put("user", "user");
    props.put("password", "passw");
    try (Connection con = DriverManager.getConnection(
      "jdbc:mysql://localhost:3306/db", props);
      Statement stmt = con.createStatement()) {
      ResultSet rs = stmt.executeQuery("SELECT * FROM USERS");
      while (rs.next()) {
        System.out.println(rs.getString("email"));
      }
    } catch (SQLException e) {
      e.printStackTrace();
    }
  }
}
```

Which of the following are TRUE statements about this program?
Choose all that apply. (Assuming the correct imports)

A. The program won't compile. `java.sql.Connection` and `java.sql.Statement` cannot be used in a try-with-resources statement.

B. The program will throw an uncaught exception if it cannot connect to the database.

C. The `ResultSet` object is never closed.

D. `java.sql.SQLException` extends from `java.lang.Exception`, so, it must be caught.

E. If the driver needed to connect to the database is not found, a `java.sql.SQLException` is thrown.

View Answer on page 288

9.3. Given:

```
 CREATE  TABLE  USERS(user_id  INTEGER  PRIMARY  KEY,  email
VARCHAR(250), active CHAR(1))
 SELECT user_id, email AS _EMAIL, active FROM USUARIO WHERE
user_id > 1
```

Which of the following are TRUE statements when executing the above query? Choose all that apply.

A. `rs.getString("email")` will get the email column.

B. `rs.getString("_EMAIL")` will get the email column.

C. `rs.getString(1)` will get the email column.

D. If column `"active"` contains the value `"0"`, `rs.getBoolean("active")` will return false.

E. `rs.getInteger("user_id")` will return the user ID as an `int`.

View Answer on page 289

9.4. Which of the following are FALSE statements? Choose all that apply.

A. A JDBC application can connect to a database using either the `java.sql.DriverManager` class or a `javax.sql.DataSource` implementation.

B. To establish a database connection, JDBC requires a database URL that has the universal format `jdbc:[databaseId]://[host][:port]/[database]` for all databases.

C. Starting from JDBC 4.0, drivers that are found in your class path are automatically loaded. (Prior to JDBC 4.0, you must manually load any drivers with the method `Class.forName()`).

D. The method `Connection.getMetaData()` returns an object that contains metadata about the database to which the `Connection` object represents a connection.

View Answer on page 290

9.5. Given:

```
public class Test {
  public static void main(String[] args) {
    Properties props = new Properties();
    props.put("user", "user");
    props.put("password", "passw");
    String s = "UPDATE USERS SET active = '1' WHERE user_id = ?";
    try (Connection con = DriverManager.getConnection(
        "jdbc:mysql://localhost:3306/db", props);
      PreparedStatement stmt = con.prepareStatement(s)) {
      stmt.setInt(1, 0); //1
      boolean b = stmt.execute();
      System.out.println(b);
    } catch (SQLException e) {
      e.printStackTrace();
    }
  }
}
```

Which of the following are TRUE statements about this program?
Choose all that apply. (Assuming the correct imports)

A. The line marked by //1 will set the value of the query parameter to 1.

B. The program will throw an exception since the update has to be committed with the instruction con.commit().

C. The program won't throw an exception but the update has to be committed to propagate the change to the database.

D. The method stmt.execute() can execute SQL UPDATE statements.

E. The boolean value returned by method stmt.execute() indicates if the SQL statement was executed successfully.

View Answer on page 291

9.6. Given:

```
public class Test {
  public static void main(String[] args) {
    Properties props = new Properties();
    props.put("user", "user");
    props.put("password", "passw");
    String sql = "UPDATE USERS SET email = ? WHERE user_id = 1";
    try (Connection con = DriverManager.getConnection(
      "jdbc:mysql://localhost:3306/db", props);
      PreparedStatement stmt = con.prepareStatement(sql)) {
      con.setAutoCommit(false);
      stmt.setString(1, "email1");
      stmt.execute();
      Savepoint s1 = con.setSavepoint();
      stmt.setString(1, "email2");
      stmt.execute();
      Savepoint s2 = con.setSavepoint();
      con.rollback(s1); //1
      //con.rollback(s2); //2
    } catch (SQLException e) {
      e.printStackTrace();
    }
  }
}
```

Which of the following are TRUE statements about this program?
Choose all that apply. (Assuming the correct imports)

A. The final value of the email column is `"email1"`.

B. The final value of the email column is `"email2"`.

C. If we remove the line `con.setAutoCommit(false);` an exception will be thrown.

D. If we comment the line marked by //1 and uncomment the line marked by //2, an exception will be thrown because no changes were made after the definition of the savepoint s2.

E. If we just uncomment the line marked by //2, an exception will be thrown.

View Answer on page 292

9.7. Which of the following are valid ways of creating a `JdbcRowSet` object? Choose all that apply.

A.
```
Connection con = DriverManager.getConnection("...");
Statement stmt = con.createStatement();
ResultSet rs = stmt.executeQuery("select * from USERS");
JdbcRowSet jdbcRs = new JdbcRowSetImpl();
```
B.
```
Connection con = DriverManager.getConnection("...");
Statement stmt = con.createStatement();
ResultSet rs = stmt.executeQuery("select * from USERS");
JdbcRowSet jdbcRs = new JdbcRowSetImpl(stmt);
```
C.
```
Connection con = DriverManager.getConnection("...");
Statement stmt = con.createStatement();
ResultSet rs = stmt.executeQuery("select * from USERS");
JdbcRowSet jdbcRs = new JdbcRowSetImpl(con);
```
D.
```
Connection con = DriverManager.getConnection("...");
Statement stmt = con.createStatement();
ResultSet rs = stmt.executeQuery("select * from USERS");
JdbcRowSet jdbcRs = RowSetProvider.newFactory().
                                        createJdbcRowSet();
```
E.
```
Connection con = DriverManager.getConnection("...");
Statement stmt = con.createStatement();
ResultSet rs = stmt.executeQuery("select * from USERS");
JdbcRowSet jdbcRs = RowSetProvider.createJdbcRowSet();
```

View Answer on page 293

9.8. Which of the following are TRUE statements? Choose all that apply.

A. `javax.sql.rowset.CachedRowSet` extends from the `javax.sql.ResultSet` interface.

B. `javax.sql.rowset.WebRowSet` and `javax.sql.rowset.QueryRowSet` are interfaces that extend from `javax.sql.RowSet` interface.

C. A `javax.sql.RowSet` object is not scrollable and updatable by default.

D. A `javax.sql.rowset.FilteredRowSet` object can manipulate and make changes to data while it is disconnected from a datasource.

View Answer on page 294

9.9. Given:

```
 CREATE   TABLE   USERS(user_id   INTEGER   PRIMARY   KEY,   email
VARCHAR(250), active CHAR(1))

public class Test {
  public static void main(String[] args) {
    Properties props = new Properties();
    props.put("user", "user");
    props.put("password", "passw");
    try (Connection con = DriverManager.getConnection(
       "jdbc:mysql://localhost:3306/db", props)) {
      CachedRowSet crs = RowSetProvider.newFactory().
                                       createCachedRowSet();
      crs.setCommand("SELECT * FROM USERS WHERE user_id = 1");
      int [] keys = {1};
      crs.setKeyColumns(keys);
      crs.execute(con); //1
      crs.updateString("email", "email1");
      crs.updateRow(); //2
    } catch (SQLException e) {
      e.printStackTrace();
    }
  }
}
```

Assuming the correct imports and that the record with user ID "1" exists, what is wrong with this program? Choose all the options that apply.

A. After line marked by //1, there must be a call to `crs.beforeFirst()`.

B. After line marked by //1, there must be a call to `crs.next()`.

C. After line marked by //2, there must be a call to `con.commit()` to persist the changes to the record.

D. After line marked by //2, there must be a call to `crs.acceptChanges()` to persist the changes to the record.

E. There is nothing wrong with the program.

View Answer on page 295

9.10. Which of the following are FALSE statements? Choose all that apply.

A. java.sql.CallableStatement is generally used to execute stored procedures.

B. The method Statement.executeUpdate(String) returns an integer representing the number of rows affected only where an UPDATE SQL statement is executed.

C. java.sql.SQLException is the only exception used by the JDBC API.

D. The method Statement.releaseSavepoint(Savepoint) takes a Savepoint object as a parameter and removes it from the current transaction.

View Answer on page 297

Practice Questions Section 10. Threads

Objectives:
- Create and use the Thread class and the Runnable interface
- Manage and control thread lifecycle
- Synchronize thread access to shared data
- Identify potential threading problems

10.1. Which of the following are valid ways to define a thread?

A. `class T extends Thread{ public void run(){} }`
B. `class T extends Runnable{ public void run(){} }`
C. `class T implements Runnable{ public void start(){} }`
D. `class T implements Thread{ public void start(){} }`

View Answer on page 301

10.2. Given:

```
public class Test extends Thread {
  public int i = 0;
  public static void main(String[] args) {
    new Test().start();
    new Test().start();
  }
  synchronized Test() {
    System.out.print(i++);
  }
}
```

What is the result when you execute this program?

A. 01

B. 00

C. One cannot be certain of the result.

D. Compilation fails.

E. An exception is thrown at runtime.

View Answer on page 302

10.3. Given:

```
public class Test extends Thread {
  private int i = 0;
  private static Object obj = new Object();

  public static void main(String[] args) {
    new Test(10).start();
    new Test(20).start();
  }

  Test(int i) {
    this.i = i;
  }

  public void run() {
    try {
      synchronized (obj) {
        System.out.print(i);
        Thread.sleep(2000);
        System.out.print(i+1);
      }
    } catch(InterruptedException e) {
      e.printStackTrace();
    }
  }
}
```

What is the result when you execute this program?

A. 10201121.

B. 10112021.

C. 20211011.

D. One cannot be certain of the result.

E. Compilation fails.

F. An exception is thrown at runtime.

View Answer on page 303

10.4. Given:

```
public class Test extends Thread {
  public static void main(String[] args) throws Exception {
    Test t = new Test();
    t.start();
    Thread.sleep(1000);
    t.interrupt();
    if(Thread.interrupted()) {
      System.out.print("3");
    }
  }

  public void run() {
    while(!Thread.interrupted()) { //1
      try {
        Thread.sleep(3000);
      } catch(InterruptedException e) {
        System.out.print("1");
      }
    }
    System.out.print("2");
  }
}
```

What is the result when you execute this program?

A. 123

B. 12

C. 2

D. Nothing is printed.

E. It prints 1 and then the loop marked by //1 is executed endlessly.

F. Compilation fails.

View Answer on page 304

10.5. Given:

```
public class Test extends Thread {
  private int i;

  public static void main(String[] args) throws Exception {
    Test t = new Test(2);
    t.start();
    t.join();
    System.out.print(10);
  }

  public void run() {
    try {
      Thread.sleep(100);
    } catch (InterruptedException e) {
      System.out.print(-1);
    }
    System.out.print(i);
  }

  public Test(int i) {
    this.i = i;
  }
}
```

What is the result when you execute this program?

A. 210

B. 102

C. -1

D. 10

E. 2

F. Compilation fails.

View Answer on page 305

10.6. Which of the following are FALSE statements? Choose all that apply.

A. A thread skips the execution of a synchronized block that is blocked by another thread.
B. A thread can acquire a lock that it already owns.
C. Multiple threads can hold the same lock at the same time.
D. A thread can hold more than one different lock at one time.

View Answer on page 306

10.7. When a thread is unable to gain regular access to shared resources and is unable to make progress; what kind of problem are we talking about?

A. A race condition.
B. A deadlock.
C. Starvation.
D. Livelock.

View Answer on page 307

10.8. When two threads each run a series of operations repeatedly until a condition becomes true, but in such a way that they cancel the others' work out just before they come to test the condition, forcing them both to restart forever; what kind of problem are we talking about?

A. A race condition.
B. A deadlock.
C. Starvation.
D. Livelock.

View Answer on page 308

10.9. Given:

```
class A {
 Object o1 = new Object();
 Object o2 = new Object();

 void m1(int i) {
   synchronized (o1) {
     System.out.print(i + 1);
     synchronized (o2) {
       System.out.print(i + 2);
     }
   }
 }

 void m2(int i) {
   synchronized (o2) {
     System.out.print(i + 10);
     synchronized (o1) {
       System.out.print(i + 20);
     }
   }
 }
}

public class Test {
 public static void main(String[] args) {
   final A a = new A();

   Thread t1 = new Thread() {
     public void run() {
       a.m1(4);
     }
   };

   Thread t2 = new Thread() {
     public void run() {
       a.m2(5);
     }
   };

   t1.start();
   t2.start();
 }
}
```

What is the result when you execute class Test?

A. 561525

B. 1525

C. 515625.

D. 155256.

E. Compilation fails.

F. None of the above.

View Answer on page 309

10.10. Given:

```
class S {
  private static S s;
  private S() {}
  public static S get() {
    if (s == null) {
      s = new S();
    }
    return s;
  }
}
public class Test {
  private static S s1;
  private static S s2;
  public static void main(String[] args) throws Exception {
    Thread t1 = new Thread() {
      public void run() {
        s1 = S.get();
      }
    };
    Thread t2 = new Thread() {
      public void run() {
        s2 = S.get();
      }
    };
    t1.start();
    t2.start();
    Thread.sleep(2000);
    System.out.println(s1 == s2);
  }
}
```

What is the result when you execute class Test?

A. It always prints true

B. It always prints false

C. Sometimes it prints true, sometimes it prints false.

D. Compilation fails.

E. An exception is thrown at run time.

View Answer on page 310

Practice Questions Section 11. Concurrency

Objectives:
- Use java.util.concurrent collections
- Apply atomic variables and locks
- Use Executors and ThreadPools
- Use the parallel Fork/Join Framework

11.1. Which of the following code fragments represent what the method ConcurrentHashMap.replace(K key, V value) does?

A.

```
synchronized(map) {
  if(!map.containsKey(key)) {
    map.put(key, value);
  }
}
```

B.

```
synchronized(map) {
  if ((map.containsKey(key) && map.get(key).equals(oldValue))
  {
    map.put(key, newValue);
  }
}
```

C.

```
synchronized(map) {
  if(map.containsKey(key)) {
    map.put(key, value);
  }
}
```

D.

```
if(map.containsKey(key)) {
  synchronized(map) {
    map.put(key, value);
  }
}
```

View Answer on page 315

11.2. Given:

```java
class P implements Runnable {
  private BlockingQueue<String> queue = null;
  public P(BlockingQueue<String> queue) {
    this.queue = queue;
  }
  public void run() {
    try {
      queue.put("1");
      Thread.sleep(1000);
      queue.put("2");
      Thread.sleep(1000);
      queue.put("3");
    } catch (InterruptedException e) {
      System.out.print("4");
    }
  }
}
class C implements Runnable {
  private BlockingQueue<String> queue = null;
  public C(BlockingQueue<String> queue) {
    this.queue = queue;
  }
  public void run() {
    try {
      System.out.print(queue.take());
      System.out.print(queue.remove());
      System.out.print(queue.poll());
    } catch (InterruptedException e) {
      System.out.print("5");
    }
  }
}
public class Test {
  public static void main(String[] args) throws Exception {
    BlockingQueue<String> queue =
                        new ArrayBlockingQueue<String>(1024);
    P p = new P(queue);
    C p = new C(queue);
    new Thread(p).start();
    new Thread(c).start();
    Thread.sleep(3000);
  }
}
```

Which of the following are TRUE statements about this program?
Choose all that apply. (Assuming the correct imports)

A. It prints 123 as a result.

B. It prints 1null2 as a result.

C. The program guarantees that 4 is always printed.

D. The program guarantees that 5 is always printed.

E. Compilation fails.

F. None of the above.

View Answer on page 316

11.3. Given:

```
public class Test {
  public static void main(String[] args) throws Exception {
    ConcurrentSkipListMap<String, String> cslm
                          = new ConcurrentSkipListMap<>();
    cslm.put("D","4");
    cslm.put("B","2");
    cslm.put("F","6");
    cslm.put("E","5");
    cslm.put("C","3");
    System.out.println(cslm.ceilingKey("A"));
    NavigableSet<String> ns = cslm.descendingKeySet();
    Iterator<String> itr = ns.iterator();
    while(itr.hasNext()){
      String s = itr.next();
      System.out.print(s);
    }
  }
}
```

What is the result when you execute this program? (Assuming the correct imports)

A. nullFEDCB

B. AFEDCB

C. nullCEFBD

D. BCEFBD.

E. BFEDCB

F. None of the above.

View Answer on page 317

11.4 Given:

```
class AI implements Runnable {
  AtomicInteger ai = null;
  AI(AtomicInteger ai) {
    this.ai = ai;
  }
  public void run() {
    System.out.println(ai.incrementAndGet());
  }
}

public class Test {
  public static void main(String[] args) {
    AtomicInteger ai = new AtomicInteger(0);
    for(int i = 0; i < 50; i++) {
      Runnable r = new AI(ai);
      Thread t = new Thread(r);
      t.start();
    }
  }
}
```

What is the result when you execute class Test? (Assuming the correct imports)

A. The program prints 1 to 50 sequentially.

B. The program prints 0 to 49 sequentially.

C. One cannot be certain of the result.

D. Compilation fails.

E. An exception is thrown at runtime.

View Answer on page 318

149

11.5. Which of the following are classes of the `java.util.concurrent.atomic` package? Choose all that apply.

A. AtomicBoolean
B. AtomicReference
C. AtomicFloat
D. AtomicBooleanFieldUpdater

View Answer on page 319

11.6. Given:

```
public class Test implements Runnable {
  int i = 0;
  public void run() {
    int r = 100/i++;
    System.out.println(r);
  }
  public static void main(String[] args) {
    ScheduledExecutorService scheduler =
      Executors.newScheduledThreadPool(1);
    final ScheduledFuture<?> sf =
      scheduler.scheduleAtFixedRate(new Test(), 1, 2,
                                    TimeUnit.SECONDS);
    scheduler.schedule(new Runnable() {
      public void run() {
        sf.cancel(true);
        System.out.println("end"); }
    }, 10, TimeUnit.SECONDS);
  }
}
```

Which of the following are TRUE statements about this program?
Choose all that apply. (Assuming the correct imports)

A. The program prints an exception, four numbers and "end".

B. The program just prints an exception.

C. The program just prints "end".

D. The method run is scheduled to execute every 10 seconds.

E. The method run is scheduled to execute every 2 seconds after a delay of 1 second.

View Answer on page 321

11.7. Which of the following code fragments makes an asynchronous call to the method M.m1() allowing to retrieve the result?

A.
```
ExecutorService executor = ...
FutureTask<String> future =
  new FutureTask<String>(new Callable<String>() {
    public String call() {
      return M.m1();
    }});
executor.execute(future);
future.get();
```
B.
```
ExecutorService executor = ...
FutureTask<String> future =
  new FutureTask<String>() {
    public String call() {
      return M.m1();
    }};
executor.execute(future);
future.get();
```
C.
```
ExecutorService executor = ...
Future<String> future
  = executor.submit(new Callable<String>() {
    public String call() {
      return M.m1();
    }});
future.get();
```
D.
```
ExecutorService executor = ...
Future<String> future

  = executor.submit(new Runnable<String>() {
    public String run() {
      return M.m1();
    }});
future.get();
```

View Answer on page 322

11.8. Which of the following are FALSE statements? Choose all that apply.

A. The only difference between `Executors.newSingleThreadExecutor()` and `Executors.newFixedThreadPool(1)` is that the former returns an `ExecutorService` that is guaranteed not to be reconfigurable to use additional threads.

B. In a thread pool created with the method `Executors.newCachedThreadPool()`, if no existing thread is available to handle a task, it will wait in the queue until a thread is available.

C. In a thread pool created with the method `Executors.newSingleThreadExecutor()`, the threads in the pool will exist until the program ends (generally when the main method ends).

D. In a thread pool created with the method `Executors.newFixedThreadPool()`, if any thread terminates due to a failure during execution, a new one will take its place if needed to execute subsequent tasks.

View Answer on page 323

11.9. Given:

```
class Operation extends RecursiveTask<Integer> {
  static final int THRESHOLD = ...
  //...

  Operation(int val1, int val2) {
    //...
  }

  protected Integer compute() {
    int r = 0;
    if(val1 + val2 <= THRESHOLD) {
      // Code to compute the operation directory
      r = ...
    } else { // Code to compute the operation in a parallel way
      // Divide the operation in two
      Operation op1 = ...
      Operation op2 = ...
      // INSERT CODE HERE
    }
    return r;
  }
}
```

Which of the following code fragments will make this program compute the operation in a real parallel way? (Assume the correct imports)

A.
```
op1.fork();
Integer r1 = op1.join();
Integer r2 = op2.compute();
r = ...
```
B.
```
op1.fork();
Integer r2 = op2.compute();
Integer r1 = op1.compute();
op1.join();
r = ...
```

C.

```
Integer r2 = op2.compute();
op1.fork();
Integer r1 = op1.join();
r = ...
```

D.

```
op1.fork();
Integer r2 = op2.compute();
Integer r1 = op1.join();
r = ...
```

View Answer on page 324

11.10. Which of the following are TRUE statements? Choose all that apply.

A. The main difference between `RecursiveTask` and `RecursiveAction` is that the latter does not return a result.

B. The method `ExecutorService.shutdownNow()` stops all currently executing tasks to shut down an `ExecutorService` but allows the waiting tasks to start.

C. The method `ForkJoinPool.submit()` supports `Callable` and `Runnable` objects.

D. The default constructor of `ForkJoinPool` uses just one of the processors available to it.

View Answer on page 325

Practice Questions Section 12. Localization

Objectives:
- Read and set the locale by using the Locale object
- Build a resource bundle for each local
- Load a resource bundle in an application
- Format text for localization by using NumberFormat and DateFormat

12.1. Which of the following are valid ways to create the Locale object for US English? Choose all that apply.

A. `Locale l = new Locale("US", "en");`
B. `Locale l = new Locale.Builder().setLanguage("en").`
`                    setRegion("US").build();`
C. `Locale l = Locale.forLanguageTag("en-US");`
D. `Locale l = Locale.ENGLISH;`

View Answer on page 329

12.2. Given:

```
public class Test {
  public static void main(String[] args) {
    Locale.setDefault(Category.FORMAT, Locale.JAPAN);
    Locale l = Locale.getDefault();

    System.out.println(l);
  }
}
```

Assuming the correct imports and that the locale of the host of the program is US English, what is the result when you execute this program?

A. en-US

B. ja-JP

C. Nothing is printed.

D. Compilation fails.

E. An exception is thrown at runtime.

View Answer on page 330

12.3. Given:

```
Locale locale = new Locale("en", "GB");
ResourceBundle labels =
                ResourceBundle.getBundle("Labels", locale);
```

and the following ResourceBundle classes:

```
Labels_en_CA
Labels_gb
Labels_en
Labels
```

Assuming that the default locale of the host of the program is US English, which class is chosen when you execute this program?

A. Labels_en_CA

B. Labels_gb

C. Labels_en

D. Labels

E. A MissingResourceException exception is thrown at runtime.

View Answer on page 331

12.4. Which of the following are TRUE statements? Choose all that apply.

A. Inside a properties file, a comment line begin with //.

B. To create a properties file for the `ResourceBundle` named `Bundle` for the French language, you should have a file named `Bundle_fr.properties`.

C. The `ResourceBundle.getBundle` method first looks for class files that match the base name and the `Locale`. If it can't find a class file, it then checks for properties files.

D. If you want to fetch the value of a property that represents an integer, you can invoke the method `ResourceBundle.getInt(String key)` to return an int type directly.

View Answer on page 332

12.5. Given:

```
public class Bundle_en extends ListResourceBundle {
  public Object[][] getContents() {
    return arr;
  }
  private Object[][] arr = {
    { "p1", "1" },
    { "p2", "2" },
    { "p3", "3" },
    { "p1", "4" }
  };
}

...

public class Test {
  public static void main(String[] args) {
    ResourceBundle rb =
    ResourceBundle.getBundle("Bundle", new Locale("en", "GB"));
    System.out.println(rb.getString("p1"));
  }
}
```

What is the result when you execute class Test? (Assuming the correct imports and that each class has its own file)

A. 1

B. 4

C. Compilation fails.

D. An exception is thrown at runtime.

View Answer on page 333

12.6. Given:

```
public class Bundle_en extends ListResourceBundle {
  public Object[][] getContents() {
    return arr;
  }
  private Object[][] arr = {
    { "p1", "1" },
    { "p2", "2" },
    { "p3", "3" },
    { "p1", new Integer(4) }
  };
}
```

. . .

```
public class Test {
  public static void main(String[] args) {
    ResourceBundle rb =
    ResourceBundle.getBundle("Bundle", new Locale("en", "GB"));
    System.out.println(rb.getString("p1"));
  }
}
```

What is the result when you execute class Test? (Assuming the correct imports and that each class has its own file)

A. 1

B. 4

C. Compilation fails.

D. An exception is thrown at runtime.

View Answer on page 334

12.7. Given:

```
public class Bundle_de_DE extends ListResourceBundle {
  public Object[][] getContents() {
    return arr;
  }
  private Object[][] arr = {
    { "p1", "1" }
  };
}
```

. . .

```
public class Bundle_my_RB extends ListResourceBundle {
  public Object[][] getContents() {
    return arr;
  }
  private Object[][] arr = {
    { "p1", "2" }
  };
}
```

. . .

```
public class RBControl extends ResourceBundle.Control {
  public List<Locale> getCandidateLocales(String baseName,
                                          Locale locale) {
    if (locale.equals(new Locale("my", "rb"))) {
      return Arrays.asList(
        Locale.GERMANY,
        locale,
        Locale.ROOT);
    } else {
      throw new RuntimeException();
    }
  }
}
```

. . .

```
public class Test {
  public static void main(String[] args) {
    Locale.setDefault(Locale.forLanguageTag("fr-FR"));
    ResourceBundle rb = ResourceBundle.getBundle(
            "Bundle", new Locale("my", "rb"), new RBControl());
    System.out.println(rb.getString("p1"));
```

```
  }
}
```

What is the result when you execute class Test? (Assuming the correct imports and that each class has its own file)

A. 1

B. 2

C. Compilation fails.

D. An exception is thrown at runtime.

View Answer on page 335

12.8. Given:

```
public class Test {
  public static void main(String[] args) {
    DecimalFormatSymbols dfs =
            new DecimalFormatSymbols(new Locale("en", "US"));

    dfs.setDecimalSeparator('|');
    dfs.setMinusSign('#');
    dfs.setPercent('?');
    String f = "000.00%";
    DecimalFormat df = new DecimalFormat(f, dfs);
    df.setGroupingSize(2);
    System.out.println(df.format(-1239.78));
  }
}
```

What is the result when you execute this program? (Assuming the correct imports)

A. #1239|78?

B. #12,39|78?

C. #12,39,78|00?

D. #123978|00?

E. Compilation fails.

F. An exception is thrown at runtime.

View Answer on page 336

12.9. Given:

```
public class Test {
  public static void main(String[] args) {
    DateFormat df = DateFormat.getDateTimeInstance(
      DateFormat.FULL,
      DateFormat.SHORT,
      new Locale("de", "DE"));
    Date d = new Date();
    System.out.println(df.format(d));
  }
}
```

Which of the following options could be the result of this program?
(Assuming the correct imports)

A. Samstag, 2. Februar 2013

B. 01:10

C. 02.02.13 01:10:23

D. 02.02.13 01:10 Uhr BRST

E. 02.02.2013 01:10

F. Samstag, 2. Februar 2013 01:10

View Answer on page 338

12.10. Given:

```
public class Test {
  public static void main(String[] args) {
    SimpleDateFormat sdf = new SimpleDateFormat(
                    "dd M yy K.m.s.S G", new Locale("en", "US"));
    Date d = new Date();
    System.out.println(sdf.format(d));
  }
}
```

Which of the following options could be the result of this program? (Assuming the correct imports)

A. 14 2 13 2.15.24.515 AD

B. 14 2 13 2.15.24.PM PST

C. 14 2 13 2.15.24.515 PM

D. 14 2 13 2.15.24.515 PST

E. 14 2 2013 2.15.24.515 AD

F. 14 2 13 14.15.24.515 AD

View Answer on page 340

Answers Section 1.
Java Class Design

1.1. The correct option is C.

Explanation:
The result is a compilation error because the constructor of class A cannot be seen by class B. It has no explicit modifier and that makes it *package private*.

There are two levels of access control:
- At the class level: It can be `public` or package-private (no explicit modifier).
- At the member level (fields and methods): It can be `private`, package-private (no explicit modifier), `protected` or `public`.

If a class is declared with the `public` modifier, the class is visible everywhere. If a class has no modifier (the default), it is visible only within its own package.

With fields and methods, you can also use the `public` modifier or no modifier with the same meaning. But in this case, there are two additional access modifiers: `private` and `protected`. The `private` modifier specifies that the member can only be accessed in its own class. The `protected` modifier has the same functionality as the package-private modifier (no modifier) and, in addition, the member can be seen by a subclass of the class that contains it (even if the subclass is in another package).

View Question on page 3

1.2. The correct option is C.

Explanation:

An instance method defined in a superclass cannot be overridden by a static method in one of its subclasses and vice versa. That is why you get a compile error in this case.

In summary, this is what happens when you define a method with the same signature in both the superclass and the subclass:

	Superclass Instance Method	**Superclass Static Method**
Subclass Instance Method	Overrides	Compile error
Subclass Static Method	Compile error	Hides

View Question on page 4

1.3. The correct option is A.

Explanation:
When dealing with overridden static methods, what we are really doing is *hiding* the method from the superclass with the one in the subclass. In other words, instance methods are overridden and static methods are hidden.

This is a subtle but important difference. The version of the hidden method that gets invoked depends on whether it is invoked from the superclass or the subclass.

In the program, we are using a reference of type A, and that is why the method invoked is the one that prints A. If we change the type of the reference to Test, the subclass version of the method will be invoked.

View Question on page 5

1.4. The correct option is D.

Explanation:
If a method overrides one of its superclass's methods, the latter can be invoked through the keyword super. For example, `super.n()`.

With `super()`, the superclass default constructor (the one with no arguments) is called. Therefore, a compilation error occurs in the program.

View Question on page 6

1.5. The correct option is D.

Explanation:

Java is a case-sensitive language, therefore, `instanceOf` is not same as `instanceof`.

The instanceof operator has the syntax:

```
reference instanceof type
```

Where in the left side we have a reference to an instance of a class, and in the right side, the type of a class. The `instanceof` operator returns `true` or `false` to indicate if the reference can be cast into the specified type and to be sure that there will be no runtime exception thrown.

View Question on page 7

1.6. The correct option is B.

Explanation:
 Polymorphism is the concept in which subclasses can define their own unique behaviors instead of sharing the behavior of their superclass. Java calls the appropriate method for the object that is referred by a variable, not by the variable's type.

In the program, we cast objB to create the variable objA with an A type, however, inside of this variable there is an object of type B, and for this reason, Java calls the method that prints Bm1 using both variables.

View Question on page 8

1.7. The correct options is E.

Explanation:
Test is not overriding the `toString()` method from `Object` because the signature of this method is wrong.

The correct signature of the `toString()` method from `Object` is:
```
public String toString()
```

This way, when the println method calls `toString()` on `Test`, the default implementation gets called and the name of the class along with the character `'@'` and the hexadecimal representation of its hash code is printed next to `"Hello "`.

View Question on page 9

1.8. The correct options are A and C.

Explanation:
Package names can have an underscore and they are written generally all in lower case to avoid conflict with the names of classes.

Option B is incorrect because package names cannot begin with a digit.

Option D is incorrect because package names cannot have hyphens.

Option E is incorrect because package names cannot contain a reserved Java keyword (in this case do).

View Question on page 10

1.9. The correct option is D.

Explanation:
Casting means converting a value or an object from one type to another. The class of the object you're casting and the class you're casting it to must be related by inheritance.

There are two types of casting:
1.Upcasting. Where a subclass object is converted to a superclass object, because a subclass object is also a superclass object. This is implicit and safe.
2.Downcasting. Where a superclass object is converted to a subclass object. This is potentially unsafe, because you could attempt to use a method that the subclass does not actually implement. This is always explicit, that is, we have to specify the type we are downcasting to.

With this in mind, the program compiles, but when is executed, a ClassCastException is thrown. The compiler only verifies that A and B are related by inheritance, but at runtime, the JVM (Java Virtual Machine) sees that the reference objA has an object of type A inside, but this class does not really have knowledge of B and the JVM throws an exception to avoid the case in which we call a method with the reference of B (objB) that the underlying object A doesn't have.

View Question on page 11

1.10. The correct options are A and E.

Explanation:
Option A is true. Numerical wrapper objects override `equals()` and `hashCode()`.

Option B is not true. The package statement is optional. A file without a package statement becomes part of the default package. A file can belong to exactly one package (one explicitly defined or the default one), which applies to all types defined in that file.

Option C is not true. A method signature includes just the method's name and its parameter list.

Option D is not true. Casting only works between parent-child types.

Option E is true. All access modifiers can be applied to constructors.

View Question on page 12

Answers Section 2.
Advanced Class Design

2.1. The correct option is E.

Explanation:
Option A is not legal because the method void `m1(String o)` is different than void `m1(Object o)`, and either the declaration is missing or the class should be marked as abstract.

Option B is not legal. `Test` is not an interface that can be implemented.

Option C is not legal because an interface must extend another interface.

Option D is incorrect because the method void `m1(String o)` either requires a body or the `abstract` modifier.

View Question on page 17

2.2. The correct options are C and E.

Explanation:

Option A is true because an abstract class can provide an implementation for certain methods (default behavior) and subclasses can provide others or override the default ones, while an interface can only define the methods.

Option B is true. Multiple interfaces can be implemented by classes.

Option C is not true. All fields inside an interface are implicitly (always) static.

Option D is true. A class can be marked as abstract even if it implements all the methods of the interface.

Option E is not true. An abstract class may have static fields and static methods. You can use these static members with a class reference as you would with any other class.

View Question on page 18

2.3. The correct option is D.

Explanation:

A variable (in any scope) that is declared as `final` means that it can be assigned only once (cannot change its value), it doesn't matter if it is not assigned when declared. When the `final` variable refers to an object, it cannot reference a different object, but the object it references can have its properties changed.

Even though `Test.t` and `obj` reference the same object, the compiler see line marked by `//2` as a reassignment, therefore, it generates an error.

View Question on page 19

2.4. The correct option is C.

Explanation:

A `final` instance variable that is not initialized when declared, must be initialized in the constructor of the class. However, when the variable is marked as `static`, it becomes a `class` variable that exists before any instance of the class where is created. This means that a `final` variable that is also `static` must be initialized in its declaration.

View Question on page 20

2.5. The correct option is D.

Explanation:
A `final` method cannot be overridden by any subclass of the class that defines it. It doesn't matter if it is `static` or not.

A `final` class can extend from another class, but it cannot be extended by another class.

View Question on page 21

2.6. The correct option is A.

Explanation:

There is nothing wrong with this program, it prints 1 when run.

An instance of the nested static class is created properly. Another way to create the instance would be new Test.A(), but in this case, the use of the enclosing class Test is not necessary since the instance is being created inside Test itself.

A static nested class cannot refer directly to instance variables or methods defined in its enclosing class. Therefore, it uses its own variable i, because it cannot see the variable i defined in Test. If we delete the variable i from class A, the compiler would generate an error.

View Question on page 22

2.7. The correct option is C.

Explanation:
The syntax to use the nested class A is correct, there is nothing wrong with the program.

The nested class can see and change the value of the `private` variable i, like any other member of the class.

View Question on page 23

2.8. The correct option is B.

Explanation:

The compiler cannot find a method named m1 that takes an int parameter because the nested class already has a method named m1. The method of the enclosing class is not visible in the inner class because it is shadowed. Shadowing is based on name rather than signature.

If we want to reference the outer class from inside the inner class we have to do it this way:

```
{NAME_OF_THE_OUTER_CLASS}.this
```

In the program, the correct instruction that prints 1 is Test.this. m1(1);

The line marked by //2 is a valid example of how to create the inner object within the outer object.

View Question on page 24

2.9. The correct option is E.

Explanation:

A compilation error is generated because two public classes cannot exist in the same file. The other options are incorrect based on this (without the public modifier in class A, the code compiles successfully and prints "B").

View Question on page 25

2.10. The correct option is B.

Explanation:

enum types can have constructors and variables.

However, the constructor for an enum must be private or package-private (no modifier), it cannot be public since you cannot invoke a constructor from outside the enum.

View Question on page 26

Answers Section 2. Advanced Class Design

Answers Section 3. Object-Oriented Design Principles

3.1. The correct option is A.

Explanation:
All variables defined in an interface are implicitly `public`, `static`, and `final`. These modifiers can be omitted.

All methods declared in an interface are implicitly `public` and `abstract`. These modifiers can be omitted also.

Therefore, the declaration of method `m()` within interface `A` generates a compile error since it can only be marked with `public` and `abstract`.

Option B is not true. An interface can extend another one.

Option C is not true. A class can implement more than one interface.

Option D is not true. A class can implement an interface and at the same time, it can extend another class.

Option E is not true since the program doesn't compile successfully.

View Question on page 31

3.2. The correct option is F.

Explanation:

All variables defined in an interface are implicitly `public`, `static`, and `final`. These modifiers can be omitted, but the fact that a variables is final means that its value cannot be changed and it must be provided in its declaration.

As the program tries to change the value of variable `i`, it generates a compile error.

View Question on page 32

3.3. The correct options are B and D.

Explanation:
The essence of the factory patterns is to encapsulate object creation. The factory method pattern encapsulates object creation by letting subclasses decide what objects to create.

Therefore:
Option A doesn't represent the factory pattern. It represents the Flyweight pattern since it uses a cache for frequently requested values.

Option B represents the factory pattern. It gets a calendar object using the default time zone and locale.

Option C doesn't represent the factory pattern. It represents the Singleton pattern because it always returns the same runtime object associated with the current Java application.

Option D represents the factory pattern. It returns a charset object for the named charset.

Option E doesn't represent the factory pattern. It represents the Adapter pattern because this method acts as bridge between array-based and collection-based APIs.

View Question on page 33

3.4. The correct option is B.

Explanation:
Option A is not true. This class doesn't represent a singleton. The goal of this pattern is to ensure that a class has only one instance at any time, to provide a global point of access, and to encapsulate the object creation. In this case, since variable t is not `final` and it is not encapsulated, it can be reassigned to `null`. Also, classes in the same package can use this class through the static variable t in addition to the method `get()`.

Option B is true according to the explanation of option A.

Option C is not true. The `private` constructor can be used inside of the class that defines it.

Option D is not true. `private` is a valid modifier for a constructor.

View Question on page 34

3.5. The correct options are B, C, and D.

Explanation:
Option A doesn't implement a "has-a" relationship. Implement an "is-a" relationship.

Option B implements a "has-a" relationship. It doesn't matter if A is a list in B.

Option C implements a "has-a" relationship. It is a bidirectional relationship, but that doesn't make it invalid.

Option D implements a "has-a" relationship. It doesn't matter if A is an interface.

Option E doesn't implement a "has-a" relationship. Classes A and B are not related.

View Question on page 35

3.6. The correct options are C and D.

Explanation:
Option A doesn't implement an "is-a" relationship. Classes A and B are not related.

Option B is not a valid implementation since it creates a cycle, which is not valid in Java.

Option C implements an "is-a" relationship through an interface.

Option D implements an "is-a" relationship. It doesn't matter if B is an abstract class.

Option E doesn't implement an "is-a" relationship. B just has a dependency on A, but this is not an "is-a" relationship.

View Question on page 36

3.7. The correct options are A and E.

Explanation:
Option A is not true. The DAO pattern is generally related to the "is-a" relationship.

Option B is true. The DAO pattern is generally related to the "is-a" relationship because it is implemented either with an interface or an abstract class.

Option C is true. It uses the Abstract Factory Pattern to create concrete DAOs implementations. It can also use an interface to define the methods to be implemented in the persistence layer.

Option D is true. A DAO uses Transfer Objects to transport data to and from its clients.

Option E is not true. DAO stands for Data Access Object.

View Question on page 37

3.8. The correct options are A and C.

Explanation:
Option A is true. `DigitalSale` inherits the list of `Product`, and since the latter is a member of the former, this is a "has-a" relationship.

Option B is not true. Each implementation of the interface would have to provide the same code for the method `calculateTotal()`.

Option C is true according to the principles *"Encapsulate what varies"* and *"Program to interfaces"*.

Option D is not true. If we make `DigitalSale` abstract, nobody could use it directly.

Option E is not true. Class `Product` has no knowledge of the other products that are part of the sale, so it wouldn't be natural to have this class calculate the total.

View Question on page 38

3.9. The correct options are A, D, and E.

Explanation:

Option A is not true. In some cases is best to use abstract classes. But sometimes, through composition and interfaces, we can achieve the same thing but in a more flexible way.

Option B is true. Since classes can implement more than one interface, we have multiple interface inheritance, that is not quite the same than multiple class inheritance but it can lead to problems also (for example, if two interfaces define the same method).

Option C is true. We can have an interface implemented through an abstract class.

Option D is not true. Class inheritance is used to provide default behavior. Interface inheritance would provide some interfaces with their implementations, but we would have to create completely new implementations, not customizing the existing ones.

Option E is not true. Class inheritance can use abstract and non-abstract classes.

View Question on page 39

3.10. The correct options are D and F.

Explanation:

Since the class Person has no relationship with any other class (String doesn't count because it is not an object with fields and methods that have functionality related to the class Person); it doesn't use composition or inheritance. *"IS A" "has a"*

Cohesion refers to the degree in which a class has a single role or responsibility. The class has low cohesion because it does a lot of unrelated functions.

The class is not correctly encapsulated, because other classes can access all of its properties and methods directly.

View Question on page 40

Answers Section 4.
Generics and Collections

4.1. The correct options are B, C, and E.

Explanation:
A generic class is defined with the following format:

```
class name<T1, T2, ..., Tn> { /* ... */ }
```

The type parameter section follows the class name and it is delimited by angle brackets (<>). It specifies type parameters (or type variables) T1, T2, ..., and Tn. A type variable can be any non-primitive type you specify: any class type, interface type, array type, or even another type variable.

In the program, class A is a generic class that defines the type variables X and Y with the restriction that Y must be an instance, subclass or implementation of X.

This way:
Option A is not valid, since B doesn't extend from C.

Option B is valid. The class can be used without any arguments types (this is called a raw type).

Option C is valid. The class can be used without any arguments types on the right side. Besides, both arguments can have the same type.

Option D is not valid. X and Y are not actual types (classes or interfaces), they are just type parameter names for the generic class.

Option E is valid. The class can be used without any type arguments types on the left side and it is legal to substitute a type parameter (X or Y) with a parameterized type (like List<Integer>, or as in the program, with A<B, C<>).

View Question on page 45

4.2. The correct option is B.

Explanation:
Starting from Java 7, you can replace the type arguments required to invoke the constructor of a generic class with an empty set of type arguments (<>) as long as the compiler can determine, or infer the type arguments from the context. This pair of angle brackets (<>), is called the diamond operator.

Java supports limited type inference for generic instance creation; you can only use type inference if the parameterized type of the constructor is obvious from the context. For this reason, it is suggested that you use the diamond operator only to initialize a variable where it is declared.

In the case of the statement `m(new ArrayList<>())`, the compiler can't really determine the type arguments and this is evaluated to `m(new ArrayList<Object>())` which doesn't correspond to `ArrayList<Integer>()`, the parameter type of method `m`.

View Question on page 46

4.3. The correct option is C.

Explanation:
A raw type is the name of a generic class or interface without any type arguments.

Raw types exist to support legacy code because classes were not generic prior to Java 5. When using raw types, you essentially get pre-generics behavior (in the case of collections, they accept elements of type Object).

For backward compatibility:
- Assigning a parameterized type to its raw type is allowed (List 12 = 11)
- If you assign a raw type to a parameterized type, you get a warning (List<Integer> 13 = 12)
- If you use a raw type to invoke generic methods defined in the corresponding generic type, you also get a warning (12. add("hello"))

However, none of these lines generate a compiler or runtime error. Generics were introduced to Java to provide tighter type checks at compile time. The program prints [1, hello, 2] because all variables reference the same object and we are skipping the types checks provided by generics.

View Question on page 47

4.4. The correct option is D.

Explanation:

Autoboxing is the automatic conversion that the Java compiler makes between the primitive types and their corresponding object wrapper classes. If the conversion goes the other way, this is called unboxing.

`11.add(1)` tries to add a primitive value to the list. Since this value is an int, the compiler converts it to `Integer` and an error is generated because the list only accepts `Long` types.

View Question on page 48

4.5. The correct option is D.

Explanation:

First, 30 and 23 are added to the list. Next, 0 is inserted between them. Then the list is duplicated and 9 is added in the fifth position, leaving 12 with [30, 0, 23, 30, 9, 0, 23]. Then a sublist from index 2 to index 5 (exclusive) is created and cleared. This sublist is a view, meaning that the returned list is backed up by the list on which subList was called, so changes in the former are reflected in the latter.

View Question on page 49

4.6. The correct option is B.

Explanation:
Set is a collection that cannot contain duplicate elements; therefore, the three elements (30, 23 and null) are only added to s2 when the object is constructed. The method addAll has no effect in this case.

View Question on page 50

4.7. The correct option is D.

Explanation:

Queue classes typically order elements in a FIFO (first in, first out) manner. However, priority queues order their elements according to their natural ordering, or by a Comparator provided at construction time. Whatever ordering is used, the head of the queue is the element that would be removed first.

The poll method removes and returns the head of the queue. The peek method returns, but do not remove, the head of the queue.

Therefore, after the for loop, q has the elements [0, 1, 2, 3, 4, 5] in that order. As the poll method removes the first two elements, the program prints [2, 3, 4, 5].

View Question on page 51

4.8. The correct options are B and D.

Explanation:
Option A is true. A map cannot contain duplicate keys, each key can map to at most one value.

Option B is not true. Map doesn't extend from Collection.

Option C is true. Maps elements can be accessed through the methods keySet, values, and entrySet.

Option D is not true. HashMap, TreeMap, LinkedHashMap, WeakHashMap and IdentityHashMap are some (but not all) of the implementations of Map.

Option E is true. With the entrySet view, it is possible to change the value associated with a key by calling a Map.Entry's setValue method during iteration (assuming the map supports value modification).

View Question on page 52

— linked hashmap
— weak — "
— Identity — ^ —
— hashmap
— TreeMap.

4.9. The correct option is D.

Explanation:

The Comparator interface has the method compare(Object obj1, Object obj2), while a class implementing the Comparable interface need to override the compareTo(Object obj) method.

Collections.sort() has two versions, one that takes a List whose elements must implement the Comparable interface, and one that takes a List and an implementation of the Comparator interface to sort that List.

Since A implements Comparator and the first version of the method is the one invoked, a compiler error is generated.

View Question on page 53

4.10. The correct option are B, D, and E.

Explanation:

Option A is not true. `SortedMap` implementations have a constructor that takes a `Comparator`.

Option B is true. `java.util.Date` implements the `Comparable` interface.

Option C is not true. A `SortedMap` maintains its entries in ascending order if an implementation of `Comparator` is not provided.

Option D is true. `TreeSet` has a `comparator` method that returns the `Comparator` used or `null` if no `Comparator` is used.

Option E is true. `Collections.binarySearch` assumes that the `List` is sorted in ascending order according to the natural ordering of its elements.

View Question on page 54

Answers Section 5.
String Processing

5.1. The correct option is A.

Explanation:

The invocations to the concat method don't change s, they produce new string objects that are not assigned to any variable, so the changes are lost. The reason behind this is that the String class is immutable, so once it is created, a String object cannot be changed. Due to this behavior, Java works with pool of strings that functions like a cache when strings are declared in this way:

```
String s = "s";
```

When strings are create with the new keyword, a new String object will be created even if it is already in the pool.

Therefore, s is never changed and when compared to "hello", the result is true because as the string is retrieved from the pool, it is the same object.

View Question on page 59

5.2. The correct option is C.

Explanation:

The first parameter is an integer referenced by %d, so there is no problem in printing 5.

The second parameter is a double referenced by %s. In this case, the toString method is called on the object the argument represents (java. lang.Double through autoboxing).

The third parameter is an integer referenced by %b. In this case, any argument different than false, will print true.

The supported conversions and format strings can be found in the documentation of java.util.Formatter.

View Question on page 60

5.3. The correct options are A, B, C, and D.

Explanation:
The format string for general, character, and numeric types have the following syntax:

`%[argument_index$][flags][width][.precision]conversion`

The optional `argument_index` is a decimal integer indicating the position of the argument in the argument list. The first argument is referenced by "1$", the second by "2$", etc.

The optional `flags` is a set of characters that modify the output format. The set of valid flags depends on the conversion.

The optional `width` is a decimal integer indicating the minimum number of characters (digits or spaces) to be written to the output.

The optional `precision` is a non-negative decimal integer usually used to restrict the number of characters.

The required `conversion` is a character indicating how the argument should be formatted. The set of valid conversions for a given argument depends on the argument's data type.

Accordingly:
Option A is valid. It represents a floating point number with a left justification of 99 characters and 5 digits of precision.

Option B is valid. It represents a floating point number with a width (left justification) of 2 characters.

Option C is valid. It represents a floating point number that is the second in the argument list and has 5 digits of precision.

Option D is valid. It represents a floating point number followed by the literal 5.

Option E is not valid. The precision cannot be a negative number.

View Question on page 61

5.4. The correct options are B, C, and E.

Explanation:

Option A is not true. Wrapper classes provide a static method named `valueOf` that converts a string to an object of that type, not the other way around.

Option B is true. `String.valueOf(i)` will convert i to a string.

Option C is true. All wrapper classes include a static `toString` method.

Option D is not true. `java.lang.Integer` provides just the `parseInt()` method. In general, all wrapper classes provide one parse method to convert a string to the primitive type the class represents.

Option E is true. A string concatenated to any primitive value will output a string.

View Question on page 62

5.5. The correct option is B.

Explanation:
The method `split(String regex)` searches for a match as specified by the string argument (a regular expression) and splits this string into an array of strings accordingly.

In the program, the regular expression represents a number followed by a space. So, the string is broken like this (elements are separated by the character "_"):

```
5_5 _aaa 7_7 _bbb 8_8 _ccc
```

Where "5 ", "7 ", and "8 " are used as separators according to the expression used, and are not taken into account.

View Question on page 63

5.6. The correct option is B.

Explanation:

The method `Pattern.compile` returns a compiled representation of a regular expression. The resulting pattern can then be used to create a `Matcher` object that can match arbitrary character sequences against the regular expression.

The program uses `"Hello Hello hello world"` as the regular expression to find in `"hello"`. Since it doesn't find it in that string, 2 is printed.

View Question on page 64

5.7. The correct option is F.

Explanation:
The expression \\d? represents zero or one digit. The greedy quantifier
? coupled with Matcher.find() give us zero-length matches. This is also
true for the quantifier *. Zero-length matches always start and end at
the same index position.

So, the result of the program is:
```
0,
1,
2, 5
3, 6
4,
5, 8
6, 5
7,
```

View Question on page 65

5.8. The correct option is C.

Explanation:

The method `replaceFirst(String replacement)` replaces the first subsequence of the input string that matches the pattern with the given replacement.

The expression \\\\ matches \\ and this is replaced by 11. \\\\ is a string with two backslashes that, as a regular expression, is interpreted as one escaped backslash (because the backslash is an escape character in regular expressions).

View Question on page 67

5.9. The correct option is D.

Explanation:
The method indexOf(String   str) returns the index of the first occurrence of the specified string, or -1 if it doesn't find one.

The method indexOf(String str, int fromIndex) returns the index of the first occurrence of the specified substring, searching forward from the specified index, or -1 if it doesn't find one.

The program finds all occurrences of 1 printing the index (starting in zero) where they were found.

View Question on page 68

5.10. The correct options are A, B, and C.

Explanation:
Option A is not true. You can specify sets of characters to search for using square brackets.

Option B is not true. \s matches just whitespace characters.

Option C is not true. The method substring(int beginIndex, int endIndex) returns a string that is a substring of the string in which is invoked. The second argument is the index of the last character **plus** one.

Option D is true. An invocation of the method String.split(regex, n) yields the same result as the method Pattern.compile(regex). split(String, n).

Option E is true. The Pattern class can accept a set of flags affecting the way the pattern is matched.

View Question on page 69

Answers Section 5. String Processing

Answers Section 6.
Exceptions and Assertions

6.1. The correct option is C.

Explanation:

Java provides many exception classes. All of them are subclasses of `Throwable`. The `throw` statement is used to throw an exception. It requires a single argument, a `Throwable` object:

```
throw ExceptionClass
```

Where `ExceptionClass` is an instance of any subclass of `Throwable`. Since an exception is class, it should be instantiated like any other, with the new operator calling one of its constructors.

Therefore, in the program, the correct way to throw the exception is: throw `new IllegalStateException()`.

View Question on page 73

6.2. The correct option is D.

Explanation:
The `throws` clause specifies a comma-separated list of all the exceptions thrown by a method. It is not mandatory to include an unchecked exception (subclasses of `RuntimeException`) in this clause. If a checked exception is thrown and it is neither caught nor declared in the throws clause, a compiler error is generated.

Therefore, the program doesn't compile because `m()` neither catches nor declares the checked exception (`Exception`) that method `m1()` throws.

We can correct the program in three ways:
- Surround the invocation of `m1()` with a `try/catch`
- Declare the exception in a throws clause in `m()`
- Throw an unchecked exception in `m1()` instead of `Exception`

View Question on page 74

6.3. The correct option is E.

Explanation:

If a method throws a given exception in its declaration, the method that override it in a subclass can only declare to throw that exception or its subclasses.

In the program, exception B extends from exception A. Then we have method m() in class C that declares exception A in its throws clause. This means that subclasses of C can only throw exceptions of type A or its subclass B. And that is what subclass D does.

However, subclasses of D now can only throw B or subclasses of it, and since class E tries to throw an exception of type A, a compile error is generated.

View Question on page 75

6.4. The correct options are C and E.

Explanation:
You can use the assert statement to test for values or conditions. The syntax is:

```
assert (boolean_expression_to_test) [: error_message]
```

If the boolean expression is false, you will get an error. If the expression returns true, there will be no error thrown. You can optionally define the error message.

If you use assert statements, you must run your program with the ea flag to activate them:

```
java -ea YourProgram.class
```

If you don't enable the support for assertions, they will be ignored.

In the program, the assertion will throw an error when variable i holds an even value or zero. Since i is defined in the for loop with an initial value of 0, this variable is the one used and an AssertionError is thrown in the first iteration when they are enabled. If they are not enabled, the program just prints all the values of i in the loop (0 to 4).

View Question on page 76

6.5. The correct option is B.

Explanation:

You can catch `AssertionError` like any other exception.

`error` will only be returned if assertions are enabled, so there is no conflict with the other `return` statement.

View Question on page 77

6.6. The correct options are A and E.

Explanation:

Option A is true. The try-with-resources statement can declare or create any number of resources that must be closed.

Option B is not true. Objects which implement `java.lang.AutoCloseable` and `java.io.Closeable` can be used as a resource.

Option C is not true. A try-with-resources statement can have `catch` or `finally` blocks like any other `try` statement.

Option D is not true. The `close` methods of the resources declared in a try-with-resources statement are called in the opposite order of their declaration.

Option E is true. In a try-with-resources statement, its `catch` and `finally` blocks are run after the resources declared have been closed.

View Question on page 78

6.7. The correct option is D.

Explanation:

In the program, both methods (read and close) throw exceptions. If an exception is thrown from the try block and one or more exceptions are thrown when trying to close one or more resources, then those exceptions thrown from the close() methods are suppressed, and the exception thrown by the try block is the one that gets caught.

You can retrieve these suppressed exceptions by calling the Throwable. getSuppressed() method from the exception thrown by the try block. It returns an array containing all of the exceptions that were suppressed. For example, in the program, the instruction inside the catch block to print Close would be:

```
System.out.println(e.getSuppressed()[0].getMessage());
```

If only the exceptions from the close() methods are thrown, the first exception is caught in the catch block and the others can be retrieved with the getSuppressed() method.

View Question on page 79

6.8. The correct option is D.

Explanation:
Starting from Java 7, a single `catch` block can handle more than one type of exception, which removes redundant code.

To use this feature, you have to specify in the catch clause the types of exceptions that it can handle, and separate each exception type with a vertical bar (|):

```
catch (ExceptionType1 | ExceptionType2 | ExceptionType3 ex) {
  ...
}
```

This way, `ex` will have a reference to the actual exception thrown at runtime.

The program doesn't compile because the syntax is incorrect, there must be only one reference to all exceptions declared in the `catch` clause.

View Question on page 80

6.9. The correct option is A.

Explanation:

In Java 7, you can rethrow an exception that is a superclass of any of the exceptions declared in the throws clause. Prior to Java 7, the compiler would have generated an error.

Since the program can either throw an exception of type A or Test, both must be declared in the throws clause for the program to compile without errors. The rules are:
- The try block throws the exception.
- There are no other preceding catch blocks that can handle the exception.
- The exception is a subclass or superclass of one of the catch block's exception parameters.

Therefore, the condition of the if statement is true and an instance of exception A is thrown. This instance is caught and rethrown as an Exception class, but at runtime, A is the class of the exception thrown and printed in the console.

View Question on page 81

6.10. The correct option is C.

Explanation:

If a `catch` block handles more than one exception type, then the `catch` parameter is implicitly `final`. So, in the program, the `catch` parameter e is `final` and therefore you cannot assign it a value within the `catch` block.

View Question on page 82

Answers Section 6. Exceptions and Assertions

Answers Section 7.
Java I/O Fundamentals

7.1. The correct option is C.

Explanation:
Everything is correct except for the fact that the method `read()` returns an `int` value, not a `byte`.

View Question on page 87

7.2. The correct options are A, B, and C.

Explanation:
Option A is not true. Classes `java.io.FileReader` and `java.io.FileWriter` are character-oriented.

Option B is not true. `PrintWriter.println` uses the line terminator for the operating system in which the program is running.

Option C is not true. `System.in` is a byte stream with no character stream features.

Option D is true. Java provides three standard streams: `System.in`, `System.out`, and `System.err`.

Option E is true. Buffered streams call native APIs only when the buffer is full (output) or empty (input).

View Question on page 88

7.3. The correct option is C.

Explanation:
`java.io.PrintWriter` and `java.io.FileWriter` are both character-oriented, that means they work with characters and convert them to bytes. They both extend from `java.io.Writer`, but `java.io.PrintWriter` in addition to the method `write()`, provides methods like `printf()`, `print()`, and `println()`. `java.io.FileWriter` in the other hand, just supports the `write()` method.

Another difference is that the methods of `java.io.FileWriter` throw a `java.io.IOException` in any case of failure, while `java.io.PrintWriter`'s methods don't throw a `java.io.IOException`, instead they set a `boolean` flag which can be obtained using the method `checkError()`.

View Question on page 89

7.4. The correct options are B, C, and D.

Explanation:
Option A is not true. `System.console` provides the method `readPassword()` that reads a password from the console with echoing disabled. `readLine()` just reads a single line of text from the console.

Option B is true. `System.console` can return `null` if console operations are not permitted, either because the OS doesn't support them or because the program was launched in a non-interactive environment.

Option C is true. The `Console` object provides input and output streams that are true character streams, through its reader and writer methods.

Option D is true. `System.out` uses the default platform encoding, while the output methods of the `Console` class use the console encoding.

View Question on page 90

7.5. The correct option is A.

Explanation:

You can create a file, append to a file, or write to a file by using the `Files.` `newOutputStream(Path, OpenOption...)` method. This method opens or creates a file for writing bytes and returns an unbuffered output stream. The method takes an optional `java.nio.file.OpenOption` parameter. If no options are specified, and the file does not exist, a new file is created. If the file exists, it is truncated. That is the behavior of the program.

View Question on page 91

7.6. The correct options are B and D.

Explanation:

Option A is not valid. There is no `readAllCharacters()` method within the class `Files`. The methods defined within class `Files` to read the entire contents of a file in one pass are `readAllBytes()` and `readAllLines()`.

Option C is not valid. This fragment of code reads from the standard input, not from a file.

View Question on page 92

7.7. The correct option is C.

Explanation:

You can create an empty file with an initial set of attributes by using the `Files.createFile()` method. In a single atomic operation, the `Files.createFile()` method checks for the existence of the file and creates that file with the specified attributes. If you do not specify any attributes, the file is created with default attributes. If the file already exists, `Files.createFile()` throws an exception. That is the reason why `"Error"` is printed.

View Question on page 93

7.8. The correct options are C, D, and E.

Explanation:
Option A is not true. `Files.newByteChannel()` and `SeekableByteChannel.` read throw an `java.io.IOException` in case of error.

Option B is not true. The program doesn't truncate the file. `SeekableByteChannel` interface allows nonsequential, or random, access to a file's contents.

Option C is true. `ByteBuffer.allocate(10)` allocates a buffer of 10 bytes.

Option D is true. `b.rewind()` is required to print the content of the buffer.

Option E is true. `b.get()` reads the byte at the buffer's current position, and then increments that position.

View Question on page 94

7.9. The correct option is A.

Explanation:
The code compiles correctly, and the file is generated but with no content. The problem is that neither the DataOutputStream nor the BufferedOutputStream resources are closed, so, the string written to the DataOutputStream is not flushed. Only FileOutputStream is closed by the try-with-resources statement. You can close only the DataOutputStream (as it wraps the BufferedOutputStream) to write the string in the file.

View Question on page 95

7.10. The correct option is only C.

Explanation:

Option A is true. The method `readPassword` has a version that takes a string as the prompt text.

Option B is true. The program never throws a `java.io.IOException`. The method `readPassword` can throw a `java.lang.IllegalFormatException` or a `java.io.IOError`

Option D is true. The `Console` object cannot be obtained from an IDE like Eclipse.

View Question on page 96

Answers Section 8.
Java File I/O (NIO.2)

8.1. The correct option is D.

Explanation:

`getName(int)` returns the path element corresponding to the specified index. The 0th element is the path element closest to the root.

`getNameCount()` returns the number of elements in the path.

`subpath(int, int)` returns the subsequence of the `Path` (not including the root element) as specified by the beginning (inclusive) and ending (exclusive) indexes.

View Question on page 101

8.2. The correct option is E.

Explanation:
All three paths reference the same file, but in distinct ways.

`equals(Object)` tests a path for equality with the given object. If the given object is not a `Path`, or is a `Path` associated with a different `FileSystem`, then this method returns `false`. Whether or not two path objects are equal depends on the file system implementation. In some cases the paths are compared without regard to case, and others are case sensitive. This method does not access the file system and the file is not required to exist.

`compareTo(Path)` compares two abstract paths lexicographically. The ordering defined by this method is provider specific, and in the case of the default provider, platform specific. This method does not access the file system and neither file is required to exist.

This way, as `p2` is not exactly the same path (although it refers to the same file) as `p1`, `p1.equals(p2)` returns `false` and `p1.compareTo(p2)` returns 19 since `p1` is lexicographically greater than `p2`. Finally, since the program is running in Windows (a case insensitive operative system), `p1.equals(p3)` returns true.

View Question on page 102

8.3. The correct option is D.

Explanation:
Option A is not true. The program compiles successfully.

Option B is not true. The methods shown in the program return `false` if the file doesn't exist, except for `Files.notExists(p)` that returns `true` in this case.

Option C is not true. The methods shown in the program return `false` if the file doesn't exist, not an exception.

Option D is true. If the existence of the file cannot be determined, `Files.exists(p)` and `Files.notExists(p)` return `false`. This means that these methods don't complement each other.

Option E is not true. The methods shown in the program return `false` if the Java Virtual Machine has insufficient privileges to read the file, not an exception.

View Question on page 103

8.4. The correct options are A, C, and D.

Explanation:

Option A is not true. The program compiles successfully. The method `delete(Path)` is declared to throw a `java.io.IOException` but this is included in the method main's `throws` clause.

Option B is true. The directory must be empty to be deleted.

Option C is not true. If the file doesn't exist, this method will throw an exception.

Option D is not true. On some operating systems, it may not be possible to remove a file when it is open and/or in use by the Java Virtual Machine or other programs.

Option E is true. The method `deleteIfExists(Path)` fails silently and it works with files and directories.

View Question on page 104

8.5. The correct options are C and D.

Explanation:

From the API documentation of method `copy`:

This method copies a file to the target file with the `options` parameter specifying how the copy is performed. By default, the copy fails if the target file already exists or is a symbolic link, except if the source and target are the *same* file, in which case the method completes without copying the file. File attributes are not required to be copied to the target file. If symbolic links are supported, and the file is a symbolic link, then the final target of the link is copied. If the file is a directory then it creates an empty directory in the target location (entries in the directory are not copied). This method can be used with the `walkFileTree` method to copy a directory and all entries in the directory, or an entire *file-tree* where required.

The options parameter may include any of the following:

Option	Description
REPLACE_EXISTING	If the target file exists, then the target file is replaced if it is not a non-empty directory. If the target is a symbolic link, the link itself is copied (and not the target of the link).
COPY_ATTRIBUTES	Attempts to copy the file attributes associated with this file to the target file. The exact file attributes that are copied is platform and file system dependent and therefore unspecified. Minimally, the `last-modified-time` is copied to the target file if supported by both the source and target file store. Copying of file timestamps may result in precision loss.

NOFOLLOW_LINKS	Symbolic links are not followed. If the file is a symbolic link, then the symbolic link itself, not the target of the link, is copied. It is implementation specific if file attributes can be copied to the new link. In other words, the COPY_ATTRIBUTES option may be ignored when copying a symbolic link.

Therefore:

Option A is not true. The instruction will copy the contents of the link (or it will fail if symbolic links are not supported).

Option B is not true. Attempts to copy the attributes associated with this file to the target file.

Option C is true. Files.copy(source, target, StandardCopyOption. REPLACE_EXISTING) copy the symbolic link itself.

Option D is true. Files.copy(source, target, LinkOption.NOFOLLOW_LINKS) copy the symbolic link itself.

Option E is not true due to options C and D.

View Question on page 105

8.6. The correct options are B, D, and E.

Explanation:

Option A is not true. Everything is fine, the program compiles successfully.

Option B is true. A `java.nio.file.NoSuchFileException` (subclass of `java.io.IOException`) is thrown and caught.

Option C is not true due to option B.

Option D is true. On the implementations where a type of attributes are not supported, a `java.lang.UnsupportedOperationException` is thrown by `Files.readAttributes()`.

Option E is true. You can set a DOS attribute using the `setAttribute(Path,` `String, Object, LinkOption...)` method as follows:

```
Files.setAttribute(f, "dos:hidden", true);
```

Where the second parameter identifies the attribute to be set and takes the form:

```
[view-name:]attribute-name
```

Where `view-name` is the name of a `FileAttributeView` that identifies a set of file attributes. If not specified, it defaults to `"basic"`, the name of the file attribute view that identifies the basic set of file attributes common to many file systems. attribute-name is the name of the attribute within the set.

View Question on page 106

8.7. The correct options are B, C, and E.

Explanation:

Option A is not true. If "C:\\temp" represents a non-existing directory, the program will execute just the method visitFileFailed of class A.

Option B is true. If "C:\\temp" represents a file, methods preVisitDirectory and postVisitDirectory won't be executed, only visitFile will be executed.

Option C is true. If "C:\\temp" represents an existing directory, the program will visit all levels of the directory tree.

Option D is not true. java.nio.file.FileVisitor is an interface. java.nio.file.SimpleFileVisitor is a class which implements the FileVisitor interface providing default implementations for all its methods.

Option E is true because the second argument represents the file visitor to invoke for each file (which are represented by java.nio.file.Path).

View Question on page 108

8.8. The correct options are B, D, and E.

Explanation:

Option A is true. If the `FileVisitor.preVisitDirectory` method returns `FileVisitResult.CONTINUE`, the current directory will be visited.

Option B is not true. If any `FileVisitor` method returns `FileVisitResult.TERMINATE`, it immediately aborts the file walking. No further file walking methods are invoked after this value is returned.

Option C is true. If the `FileVisitor.postVisitDirectory` method returns `FileVisitResult.SKIP_SIBLINGS`, no further sibling directories will be visited.

Option D is not true. If the `FileVisitor.preVisitDirectory` method returns `FileVisitResult.SKIP_SUBTREE`, the current directory and all its elements will be skipped.

Option E is not true. `FileVisitResult.SKIP_NEXT_FILE` doesn't exist.

View Question on page 110

8.9. The correct options are A and B.

Explanation:

The glob expression "[!f.]?{z[A-E]}" represents strings beginning with any character except "f" or ".", followed by any character and ending in "z" followed by "A", "B", "C", "D", or "E" (For both the glob and regex syntaxes, the matching details, such as whether the matching is case sensitive, are implementation-dependent and therefore not specified, for example, the Windows implementation is not case sensitive).

Option A will match the glob expression. It starts with "!", that is not "f" or ".". It is followed by "h" and then "zA".

Option B will match the glob expression. It starts with ",", that is not "f" or ".". It is followed by "9" and then "zE".

Option C will not match the glob expression. It starts with "f".

Option D will not match the glob expression. It ends with "F", that is outside the range A-E.

Option E will not match the glob expression. One character is missing, either before (to represent "[!f.]") or after (to represent "?") character "k".

View Question on page 111

8.10. The correct options are A, D, and E.

Explanation:

Option A is true. The watch service exits when either the thread exits or when the service is closed (by invoking its `close()` method).

Option B is not true. Path is not a class, it is an interface and it does extend from the `java.nio.file.Watchable` interface.

Option C is not true. `java.nio.file.StandardWatchEventKinds` supports the following event types:

- `ENTRY_CREATE` - A directory entry is created.
- `ENTRY_DELETE` - A directory entry is deleted.
- `ENTRY_MODIFY` - A directory entry is modified.
- `OVERFLOW` - Indicates that events might have been lost or discarded. You do not have to register for the `OVERFLOW` event to receive it.

Option D is true. A watch key can have the `Invalid` state that indicates that the key is no longer active, when for example, the watched directory becomes inaccessible.

Option E is true. Once a watch key acquires the `Signaled` state, it is no longer in the `Ready` state until its reset method is invoked and it cannot receive any further events.

View Question on page 112

Answers Section 9.
Building Database
Applications with JDBC

9.1. The correct option is B.

Explanation:
First, establish a connection with the data source you want to use. A data source can be a database, a legacy file system, or some other source of data with a corresponding JDBC driver.

Second, create a `Statement` object from the connection object. `Statement` is an interface that represents a SQL statement.

Then, to execute a query, call an execute method from the `Statement` object. This will return a `ResultSet` object.

From the `ResultSet` object, retrieve the results.

When you are finished, close all the objects to release the resources used.

View Question on page 117

9.2. The correct options are D and E.

Explanation:

Option A is not true. `java.sql.Connection`, `java.sql.Statement`, and `java.sql.ResultSet` implement the `java.lang.AutoCloseable` interface.

Option B is not true. The program will throw a `java.sql.SQLException` (a checked exception) if it cannot connect to the database.

Option C is not true. When you call close the `Statement` object (in this case is closed automatically), its `ResultSet` objects are also closed.

Option D is true. `java.sql.SQLException` extends from `java.lang.Exception`.

Option E is true. The program will throw a `java.sql.SQLException` if the driver needed to connect to the database is not found.

View Question on page 118

9.3. The correct options are B and D.

Explanation:
Option A is not true. The label specified with the SQL AS clause is used.

Option B is true according to the explanation of option A.

Option C is not true. The index used as an argument starts at 1, so `rs.getString(1)` will get the user ID as an String.

Option D is true. `"0"` will return `false`, `"1"` will return true.

Option E is not true. The correct method invocation is `rs.getInt("user_id")`.

View Question on page 119

9.4. The only correct option is B.

Explanation:

Option A is true. A JDBC application can connect to a database using either the `java.sql.DriverManager` class or a `javax.sql.DataSource` implementation.

Option B is not true. A database connection URL is a string that a JDBC driver uses to connect to a database. It can contain information such as where to search for the database, the name of the database to connect to, and configuration properties. The exact syntax of a database connection URL is specified by the database, it is not universal.

Option C is true. Starting from JDBC 4.0, drivers that are found in your class path are automatically loaded (only JDBC 4 drivers).

Option D is true. The method `Connection.getMetaData()` returns an object that contains metadata about the database.

View Question on page 120

9.5. The only correct option is D.

Explanation:

Option A is not true. The first argument of the method represents the parameter number of the query starting from 1. The second argument is the parameter value to set.

Option B is not true. The program won't throw an exception if `con.commit()` is not called. In fact, when a connection is created, it is in auto-commit mode. This means that each individual SQL statement is treated as a transaction and is automatically committed right after it is executed.

Option C is not true according to the explanation of option B.

Option D is true. The method `stmt.execute()` can execute any kind of SQL statement.

Option E is not true. Since the method `stmt.execute()` can execute any kind of SQL statement, it returns true if the first result is a `ResultSet` object; false if the first result is an update count or there is no result.

View Question on page 121

9.6. The correct options are A, C, and E.

Explanation:

Option A is true. The value of the email column is reverted to `"email1"` because that was the value of the column when the savepoint s1 was created.

Option B is not true due to the explanation of option A.

Option C is true. A transaction ends either with a commit or a rollback, if the auto-commit mode is set, the transaction ends with each call to `stmt.execute()` and an exception is thrown when trying to create a savepoint.

Option D is not true. No exception is thrown; the rollback is made leaving the value `"email2"`.

Option E is true. A transaction ends either with a commit or a rollback. Any savepoints that have been created in a transaction are automatically released and become invalid when the transaction is committed, or when the entire transaction is rolled back. Since a rollback is issued by savepoint s1, savepoint s2 becomes invalid and an exception is thrown when is used.

View Question on page 122

9.7. The correct options are A, C, and D.

Explanation:
Option A is valid. You can create a `JdbcRowSet` object by using the reference implementation default constructor.

Option B is not valid. You cannot create a `JdbcRowSet` object by passing to the constructor of the reference implementation a `Statement` object.

Option C is valid. You can create a `JdbcRowSet` object by using the reference implementation constructor that takes a `Connection` object.

Option D is valid. You can create a `JdbcRowSet` object by using an instance of `RowSetFactory`, which is created from the class `RowSetProvider`.

Option E is not valid since you cannot create a `JdbcRowSet` object directly from the class `RowSetProvider`.

View Question on page 123

9.8. The correct options are A and D.

Explanation:

Option A is true. `javax.sql.rowset.CachedRowSet` and others interfaces that extend the `javax.sql.RowSet`, also extends from the `javax.sql.ResultSet` interface.

Option B is not true. `javax.sql.rowset.QueryRowSet` doesn't exist. The following interfaces extend the `javax.sql.RowSet` interface:

- `javax.sql.rowset.JdbcRowSet`
- `javax.sql.rowset.CachedRowSet`
- `javax.sql.rowset.WebRowSet`
- `javax.sql.rowset.JoinRowSet`
- `javax.sql.rowset.FilteredRowSet`

Option C is not true. A `javax.sql.RowSet` object is scrollable and updatable by default. If a driver for a DBMS does not add the ability to scroll or update result sets, you can use a `javax.sql.RowSet` object to do it.

Option D is true. `javax.sql.rowset.FilteredRowSet` extends from `javax.sql.rowset.CachedRowSet`, so it can manipulate and make changes to data while it is disconnected from a datasource.

View Question on page 124

9.9. The correct options are B and D.

Explanation:

In the program, the following line of code sets the command property with a query that produces a ResultSet object containing the record with user ID "1":

```
crs.setCommand("SELECT * FROM USERS WHERE user_id = 1");
```

Then, the program sets a key column. Key columns are essentially the same as a primary key because they indicate one or more columns that uniquely identify a row. The difference is that a primary key is set on a table in the database, whereas key columns are set on a particular RowSet object. With the following lines, the program sets the first column of the query (user_id) as a key column:

```
int [] keys = {1};
crs.setKeyColumns(keys);
```

The program executes the query with the statement crs.execute(con). Then, to update the record, the cursor must point to it. This can be done with crs.next(), not with crs.beforeFirst() that moves the cursor to the front of the ResultSet object, just before the first row.

Finally, after the email column is modified, the call to crs.updateRow() must be accompanied with crs.acceptChanges().

There is a major difference between making changes to a JdbcRowSet object and making changes to a CachedRowSet object. Because a JdbcRowSet object is connected to its data source, the methods updateRow, insertRow, and deleteRow can update both the JdbcRowSet object and the data source. In the case of a disconnected RowSet object, these methods update the data stored in the CachedRowSet object's memory but cannot affect the data source. A disconnected RowSet object must call the method acceptChanges in order to save its changes to the data source; `con.commit()` won't do it.

View Question on page 125

9.10. The correct options are B and D.

Explanation:

Option A is true. `java.sql.CallableStatement` is used to execute stored procedures that may contain both input and output parameters.

Option B is not true. The method `Statement.executeUpdate(String)` returns an integer representing the number of rows affected for INSERT, DELETE, and UPDATE SQL statements.

Option C is true. `java.sql.SQLException` is the only exception used by the JDBC API. If you want to know what the cause of the exception was, you have to look into the exception for the error code or the error message.

Option D is not true. The method `Connection.releaseSavepoint(Savepoint)` takes a `Savepoint` object as a parameter and removes it from the current transaction. The method `Statement.releaseSavepoint(Savepoint)` doesn't exist.

View Question on page 126

Answers Section 10. Threads

10.1. The correct option is A.

Explanation:
There are two ways to do define a thread:

- Interface Runnable. The Runnable interface defines the method run() to contain the code executed in the thread. A Runnable object is passed to the Thread constructor.
- Subclass Thread. The Thread class itself implements Runnable, though its run() method does nothing. An application can subclass Thread, providing its own implementation of method run().

Therefore:

Option B is incorrect, Runnable is an interface.

Option C is incorrect, Runnable doesn't have the method start().

Option D is incorrect, Thread is not an interface.

View Question on page 131

10.2. The correct option is D.

Explanation:
Constructors cannot be synchronized; using the `synchronized` keyword with a constructor is a compile error. Synchronizing constructors doesn't make sense, because only the thread that creates an object should have access to it while it is being constructed.

View Question on page 132

10.3. The correct option is D.

Explanation:

Synchronization is built around a mechanism known as the intrinsic lock or monitor lock. Every object has an intrinsic lock associated with it. When a thread invokes a synchronized method, it automatically acquires the intrinsic lock for that method's object and releases it when the method returns. Another way to create synchronized code is with `synchronized` blocks. Unlike synchronized methods, `synchronized` blocks must specify the object that provides the intrinsic lock.

In the program, a static variable that is shared across all instances of class `Test` (`obj`) is used to synchronize the block inside method `run`. This means that only one thread at a time can access the block. **If we assume that the thread that has the value 10 will start before the other thread**, `10` and `11` are printed and immediately after that, the first thread release the lock so the second thread can execute the block and print `20` and `21`.

However, **we cannot assume that 100% of the time the first thread started will begin its execution before the other thread**. Java leaves certain aspects of the thread's scheduling to the JVM implementation. For example, threads at the same priority can be scheduled to run using a round robin or a time-sliced algorithm. Having a multiple processor machine executing the program, can also have an effect in the output. That's the reason option D is the correct answer.

View Question on page 133

10.4. The correct option is E.

Explanation:
A thread sends an interruption by invoking the method interrupt on the Thread object to be interrupted.

When a thread is interrupted, methods such as Thead.sleep() cancel their current operation and return immediately throwing an InterruptedException. The interrupt mechanism is implemented using an internal flag known as the interrupt status. Invoking Thread.interrupt sets this flag. When a thread checks for an interruption by invoking the static method Thread.interrupted, the interrupt status is cleared.

However, if a method exits by throwing an InterruptedException, it also clears the interrupt status.

In the program, the thread t is started and the thread running main() is put to sleep enough time to interrupt t while this is sleeping. This way, an InterruptedException is thrown printing 1. However, the interrupted status is cleared and the loop condition is never false, so 2 is never printed.

The Thread.interrupted() statement in method main checks if the thread running main was interrupted, not thread t, so the program never prints 3.

View Question on page 134

10.5. The correct option is A.

Explanation:

The join method allows one thread to wait for the completion of another. If t is a Thread, t.join() causes the current thread to wait (pause its execution) until t terminates.

In the program, when t is started, is put to sleep to give chance to t.join() to execute. When this happens, main's thread is paused until t.run() prints "2" and then, when execution is resumed for main, it prints "10".

View Question on page 135

10.6. The correct options are A and C.

Explanation:

Option A is not true. A thread that tries to enter a synchronized block that is blocked by another thread waits for that thread to release the lock, so it can acquire it and execute the block.

Option B is true. A thread can acquire a lock that it already owns. Allowing a thread to acquire the same lock more than once enables reentrant synchronization. This describes a situation where synchronized code, directly or indirectly, invokes a method that also contains synchronized code, and both sets of code use the same lock.

Option C is not true. A thread cannot acquire a lock owned by another thread.

Option D is true. A thread can hold multiple locks by nesting synchronized blocks where each one has a different lock.

View Question on page 136

10.7. The correct option is C.

Explanation:

Starvation describes a situation where a thread is unable to gain regular access to shared resources and is unable to make progress. This happens when shared resources are made unavailable for long periods by other threads. For example, when an object provides a synchronized method that often takes a long time to return, if one thread invokes this method frequently, other threads that also need frequent synchronized access to other methods of the same object will often be blocked because all methods share the same lock on the object.

View Question on page 137

10.8. The correct option is D.

Explanation:

A thread often acts in response to the action of another thread. If the other thread's action is also a response to the action of another thread, then a livelock may result. As with deadlock, livelocked threads are unable to make further progress, except that they are not blocked, they are simply responding to each other constantly to resume work. In a few words, if a system repeats itself to no effect, it is a livelock.

View Question on page 138

10.9. The correct option is F.

Explanation:

The program prints 5, then 15 and then a deadlock is produced because t1 acquires a lock on o1 while executing m1() and t2 acquires a lock on o2 while executing m2(). This way, both will be waiting for each other to release lock on o2 and o1 to proceed, which will never happen.

A deadlock describes a situation where two or more threads are blocked forever, waiting for each other. If you see nested synchronized blocks, calling one synchronized method from other, or trying to get lock on different objects, watch out for a deadlock situation.

View Question on page 139

10.10. The correct option is C.

Explanation:

Class s represents a Singleton. But the implementation shown is not thread-safe. This is what can happen:

1. t1 enters get() for the first time and sees that s is null, thereby, the condition is true.
2. Before the object is instantiated, t1 is paused and t2 enters the method.
3. t2 enters get() and sees that s is still null.
4. t2 instantiate s and returns it.
5. t1 resume its execution, instantiate s again and returns it.

After all this, we have two instances of class s, which violates the purpose of the Singleton pattern.

This problem is known as race condition. A race condition occurs when two threads access a shared variable at the same time. The first thread reads the variable, and the second thread reads the same value from the variable. Then the first thread and second thread perform their operations on the value, and they race to see which thread can write the value last to the shared variable. The value of the thread that writes its value last is preserved, because the thread is writing over the value that the previous thread wrote.

In this case, we can solve the problem in two ways:
- Initialize s in its declaration.
- Synchronize the whole get method.

View Question on page 141

Answers Section 11. Concurrency

11.1. The correct option is C.

Explanation:

Option A is not true. The code fragment represents what method `ConcurrentHashMap.putIfAbsent(K key, V value)` does (if the specified key is not already associated with a value, associate it with the given value).

Option B is not true. The code fragment represents what method `ConcurrentHashMap.replace(K key, V oldValue, V newValue))` does (it replaces the entry for a key only if currently mapped to a given value).

Option C is true. The code fragment represents what method `ConcurrentHashMap.replace(K key, V value)` does (it replaces the entry for a key only if currently mapped to some value).

Option D is not true. The code doesn't resolve concurrency problems because two different threads can be inside the if block at the same time.

View Question on page 145

315

11.2. The correct option is F.

Explanation:
BlockingQueue methods come in four forms, with different ways of handling operations that cannot be satisfied immediately, but may be satisfied at some point in the future: one throws an exception, the second returns a special value (either null or false, depending on the operation), the third blocks the current thread indefinitely until the operation can succeed, and the fourth blocks for only a given maximum time limit before giving up. These methods are summarized in the following table:

	Throws exception	Special value	Blocks	Times out
Insert	add(e)	offer(e)	put(e)	offer(e, time, unit
Remove	remove()	poll()	take()	poll(time, unit)
Examine	element()	peek()	*Not Applicable*	*Not Applicable*

The calls to Thread.sleep() in the first thread (P class) between each put method call will cause the other thread (C class) to block while waiting for objects in the queue. So, the second thread will throw an java.util.NoSuchElementException due to the call to queue.remove(), an exception that is not caught. This way, "2", "3", and "5" are never printed. Neither is "4" since put() or sleep() methods never throw an InterruptedException.

View Question on page 146

11.3. The correct option is E.

Explanation:

ConcurrentNavigableMap is a subinterface of ConcurrentMap that supports approximate matches. The standard general-purpose implementation of ConcurrentNavigableMap is ConcurrentSkipListMap, which is a concurrent analog of TreeMap. The map is sorted according to the natural ordering of its keys, or by a Comparator provided at map creation time, depending on which constructor is used.

The method ConcurrentSkipListMap.ceilingKey(String key) returns the least key greater than or equal to the given key, or null if there is no such key.

The method ConcurrentSkipListMap.descendingKeySet() returns a reverse order NavigableSet view of the keys contained in this map. The set's iterator returns the keys in descending order. The set is backed by the map, so changes to the map are reflected in the set, and vice-versa.

Therefore, in the program, since the map is sorted according to the natural ordering of its keys, ceilingKey("A") returns "B" and the elements are printed in descending order, "FEDCB".

View Question on page 148

11.4. The correct option is A.

Explanation:

The class `java.util.concurrent.atomic.AtomicInteger` represents an int value that is updated atomically. This class is generally used as an atomically incremented counter. It cannot be used as a replacement for a `java.lang.Integer`, however, this class does extend `Number` to allow uniform access by tools and utilities that deal with numerically-based classes.

The method `incrementAndGet()` atomically increments by one the current value and then returns it. As the same object is shared by all the threads, the program prints the values from 1 to 50 sequentially.

View Question on page 149

11.5. The correct options are A and B.

Explanation:

These are the classes inside the `java.util.concurrent.atomic` package:

Class	Description
AtomicBoolean	A `boolean` value that may be updated atomically.
AtomicInteger	An `int` value that may be updated atomically.
AtomicIntegerArray	An `int` array in which elements may be updated atomically.
AtomicIntegerFieldUpdater\<T\>	A reflection-based utility that enables atomic updates to designated `volatile int` fields of designated classes.
AtomicLong	A `long` value that may be updated atomically.
AtomicLongArray	A `long` array in which elements may be updated atomically.
AtomicLongFieldUpdater\<T\>	A reflection-based utility that enables atomic updates to designated `volatile long` fields of designated classes.
AtomicMarkableReference\<V\>	An `AtomicMarkableReference` maintains an object reference along with a mark bit that can be updated atomically.
AtomicReference\<V\>	An object reference that may be updated atomically.

AtomicReferenceArray<E>	An array of object references in which elements may be updated atomically
AtomicReferenceFieldUpdater<T,V>	A reflection-based utility that enables atomic updates to designated `volatile` reference fields of designated classes.
AtomicStampedReference<V>	An `AtomicStampedReference` maintains an object reference along with an integer "stamp" that can be updated atomically.

There are no atomic classes for float and double types. You can hold floats using `Float.floatToIntBits(float)` and `Float.intBitsToFloat(int)` conversions, and doubles using `Double.doubleToLongBits(double)` and `Double.longBitsToDouble(long)` conversions.

View Question on page 150

11.6. The correct options are C and E.

Explanation:

The method scheduleAtFixedRate(Runnable command, long initialDelay, long period, TimeUnit unit) creates and executes a periodic action that becomes enabled first after the given initial delay, and subsequently with the given period; that is, executions will start after initialDelay then initialDelay+period, then initialDelay + 2 * period, and so on.

However, if any execution of the task throws an uncaught exception, subsequent executions are suppressed.

This is what happens in the program. After one second, the method run() is executed and since i++ evaluates to 0, an uncaught exception is thrown. So, the task is cancelled, and after ten seconds (due to the second scheduled task), sf.cancel(true) doesn't have any effect and "end" is printed.

View Question on page 151

11.7. The correct options are A and C.

Explanation:
Option A is correct. The FutureTask class is an implementation of Future that also implements Runnable, so it may be executed by an Executor.

Option B is not correct. The FutureTask class doesn't have a default constructor nor a call method. It has one constructor that takes an implementation of Callable and another that takes an implementation of Runnable and the type of the Result.

Option C is correct. The method submit accepts Callable objects that returns a Future object, which is used to retrieve the return value.

Option D is not correct. The method submit also accepts Runnable objects and returns a Future object representing that task. However, the Future's get method will return null upon successful completion. Besides, the method run has a void return type.

View Question on page 152

11.8. The correct options are B and C.

Explanation:

Option A is true. The only difference between `Executors.`
`newSingleThreadExecutor()` and `Executors.newFixedThreadPool(1)` is
that the former returns an `ExecutorService` that is guaranteed not to be
reconfigurable to use additional threads.

Option B is not true. In a thread pool created with the method `Executors.`
`newCachedThreadPool()`, if no existing thread is available to handle a
task, a new thread will be created.

Option C is not true. In a thread pool created with the method `Executors.`
`newSingleThreadExecutor()`, the threads in the pool will exist until the
method shutdown is explicitly called. When this method is called, the
`ExecutorService` will not shut down immediately, but it will no longer
accept new tasks, and once all threads have finished current tasks, it
shuts down.

Option D is true. In a thread pool created with the method `Executors.`
`newFixedThreadPool()`, if any thread terminates due to a failure during
execution, a new one will take its place if needed to execute subsequent
tasks.

View Question on page 153

11.9. The correct option is D.

Explanation:
The method join() returns the result of the computation when it is done. It blocks the program until the answer is ready. So, the order in which join() and fork() are called is important.

Option A is not correct. The code of this option blocks the program until the result of op1 is returned and then, it computes op2. There is no parallelism here.

Option B is not correct. The code of this option computes both results sequentially. Besides, this is not the correct way to use fork/join.

Option C is not correct. The code of this option computes op2 first and then block the program until the result of op1 is returned. Again, there is no parallelism here.

Option D is the right way to do it.

View Question on page 154

11.10. The correct options are A and C.

Explanation:

Option A is true. `RecursiveAction` does not return a result while `RecursiveTask` does.

Option B is not true. The method `ExecutorService.shutdownNow()` attempts to stop all actively executing tasks, halts the processing of waiting tasks, and returns a list of the tasks that were awaiting execution.

Option C is true. The method `ForkJoinPool.submit()` supports `Callable` and `Runnable` objects.

Option D is not true. The default constructor of `ForkJoinPool` uses all of the processors available to it.

View Question on page 156

Answers Section 12.
Localization

12.1. The correct options are B and C.

Explanation:
Option A is not valid. `Locale l = new Locale("en", "US")` is the valid way to use the constructor, first the language, then the region.

Option D is not valid. `Locale.ENGLISH` references just the locale object for English, but not for US. The correct constant is `Locale.US`.

View Question on page 161

12.2. The correct option is A.

Explanation:

Set by the Java Virtual Machine when it starts up, the default `Locale` corresponds to the locale of the host platform. To determine the default `Locale` of your Java Virtual Machine, invoke the `Locale.getDefault()` method. To set the default Locale, invoke the `Locale.setDefault(Locale)` method.

It also is possible to independently set the default `Locale` for two types of uses: the format setting is used for formatting resources, and the display setting is used in menus and dialogs. Introduced in Java 7, the `Locale.getDefault(Locale.Category)` method takes a `Locale.Category` parameter. Passing the `FORMAT` enum to the `getDefault(Locale.Category)` method returns the default locale for formatting resources. Similiarly, passing the `DISPLAY` enum returns the default `Locale` used by the user interface. The corresponding `setDefault(Locale.Category, Locale)` method allows setting the Locale for the desired category.

View Question on page 162

12.3. The correct option is C.

Explanation:

If a ResourceBundle class for the specified Locale does not exist, getBundle tries to find the closest match. For example, if Labels_it_IT is the desired class and the default Locale is en_US, getBundle will look for classes in the following order:

```
Labels_it_IT
Labels_it
Labels_en_US
Labels_en
Labels
```

getBundle looks for classes based on the default Locale before it selects the base class (Labels). If getBundle fails to find a match in the preceding list of classes, it throws a MissingResourceException. To avoid throwing this exception, you should always provide a base class with no suffixes.

View Question on page 163

12.4. The correct options are B and C.

Explanation:

Option A is not true. Inside a properties file, a comment line begins with #.

Option B is true. To create a properties file for the ResourceBundle named Bundle for the French language, you should have a file named Bundle_fr.properties.

Option C is true. The ResourceBundle.getBundle method first looks for a class file that matches the base name and the Locale. If it can't find a class file, it then checks for properties files.

Option D is not true. The method ResourceBundle.getInt(String key) doesn't exist. You have to use either ResourceBundle.getString(String key) or ResourceBundle.getObject(String key) to fetch the value of a property.

View Question on page 164

12.5. The correct option is B.

Explanation:
A ListResourceBundle is backed up by a class file. The class name is constructed by appending the language and country code to the base name of the ListResourceBundle. Inside the class, a two-dimensional array is initialized with the key-value pairs.

If there are two entries with the same key, the last one defined is always fetched for that key.

View Question on page 165

12.6. The correct options is D.

Explanation:

In a ListResourceBundle class, the keys must be String objects, but the values can be any type of object. To retrieve an object of a type different than String, the method getObject should be invoked. Since getObject returns an Object, it should be casted to the expected type.

Therefore, the program throws a ClassCastException since a java.lang.Integer cannot be cast to java.lang.String.

View Question on page 166

12.7. The correct option is A.

Explanation:

ResourceBundle.Control defines a set of callback methods that are invoked by the ResourceBundle.getBundle method during the bundle loading process. In other words, a ResourceBundle.Control collaborates with that method for loading resource bundles.

The ResourceBundle.Control.getCandidateLocales method returns a list of the Locale objects as candidate locales for the base name and locale. This method is overridden to implement specific behavior, as in the program, where is overridden to find the locale "de_DE" instead of the locale "my_RB" when we ask for the latter.

View Question on page 167

12.8. The correct option is D.

Explanation:

The DecimalFormatSymbols class changes the symbols that appear in the formatted numbers produced by the format method; including the decimal separator, the grouping separator, the minus sign, and the percent sign, among others.

Regarding the symbols you can use to format numbers, the following table summarizes them:

Symbol	Description
0	a digit
#	a digit (if the digit is zero, it is not shown)
.	placeholder for decimal separator
,	placeholder for grouping separator
E	separates mantissa and exponent for exponential formats
;	separates formats
-	default negative prefix
%	multiply by 100 and show as percentage
?	multiply by 1000 and show as per mille
¤	currency sign; if doubled, replaced by international currency symbol; if present in a pattern, the monetary decimal separator is used instead of the decimal separator
X	any other characters can be used in the prefix or suffix
'	used to quote special characters in a prefix or suffix

Therefore, in the program we change the decimal separator, the minus sign, and the percent symbol. We also set a grouping size of two (the default is three to separate thousands) but since in the format string we don't define a separator, this option is not used. As we are formatting a negative percentage number, it is multiplied by 100 yielding

-123978.00%, but showing it as #123978|00?

View Question on page 169

12.9. The correct option is F.

Explanation:
The formatter created with the getDateTimeInstance method display a date and time in the same String. The first parameter is the date style, and the second is the time style. The third parameter is the Locale.

The predefined formatting styles that the DateFormat class provides are:
- DEFAULT
- SHORT
- MEDIUM
- LONG
- FULL

The following table shows how dates are formatted for each style with the U.S. and German locales:

Style	U.S. Locale	German Locale
DEFAULT	Feb 14, 2013	14.02.2013
SHORT	2/14/13	14.02.13
MEDIUM	Feb 14, 2013	14.02.2013
LONG	February 14, 2013	14. Februar 2013
FULL	Thursday, February 14, 2013	Donnerstag, 14. Februar 2013

The following table shows how times are formatted for each style with the U.S. and German locales:

Style	U.S. Locale	German Locale
DEFAULT	1:30:01 AM	01:30:01
SHORT	1:30 AM	01:30
MEDIUM	1:30:01 AM	01:30:01

| LONG | 1:30:01 AM PST | 01:30:01 PST |
| FULL | 1:30:01 AM PST | 01:30 Uhr PST |

Therefore, only option F is correct.

Options A and B are wrong because the date and time should appear in the same String.

Option C shows the SHORT style for date and the MEDIUM style for time.

Option D shows the SHORT style for date and the FULL style for time.

Option E shows the DEFAULT (or MEDIUM) style for date and the SHORT style for time.

View Question on page 170

12.10. The correct option is A.

Explanation:

The `SimpleDateFormat` class is locale-sensitive. If you instantiate `SimpleDateFormat` without a `Locale` parameter, it will format the date and time according to the default `Locale`. Both, the pattern and the `Locale` used, determine the format. For the same pattern, `SimpleDateFormat` may format a date and time differently if the `Locale` varies.

The following table shows the symbols we can use to format dates:

Symbol	Meaning	Presentation	Example
G	era designator	Text	AD
y	year	Number	2009
M	month in year	Text & Number	July & 07
d	day in month	Number	10
h	hour in am/pm (1-12	Number	12
H	hour in day (0-23)	Number	0
m	minute in hour	Number	30
s	second in minute	Number	55
S	millisecond	Number	978
E	day in week	Text	Tuesday
D	day in year	Number	189
F	day of week in month	Number	2 (2nd Wed in July)
w	week in year	Number	27
W	week in month	Number	2
a	am/pm marker	Text	PM
k	hour in day (1-24)	Number	24
K	hour in am/pm (0-11	Number	0

z	time zone	Text	Pacific Standard Time
Z	time zone (RFC 822)	Text	-0500
X	time zone (ISO 8601)	Text	-05;-0500;-05:00
'	escape for text	Delimeter	(none)
'	single quote	Literal	'

The number of symbol letters you specify also determines the format. For example, if the "MM" pattern results in "01", then the "MMMM" pattern generates "January". The following table summarizes these rules:

Presentation	Number of Symbols	Result
Text	1 - 3	abbreviated form, if one exists
Text	>= 4	full form
Number	minimum number of digits is required	shorter numbers are padded with zeros (for a year, if the count of 'y' is 2, then the year is truncated to 2 digits)
Text & Number	1 - 2	number form
Text & Number	3	text form

Therefore, only option A is correct.
Option B represents the pattern dd M yy K.m.s.a zz.
Option C represents the pattern dd M yy K.m.s.S a.
Option D represents the pattern dd M yy K.m.s.S zz.
Option E represents the pattern dd M yyyy K.m.s.S G.
Option F represents the pattern dd M yy k.m.s.S G.

View Question on page 171

Finally

Well, that's all. 120 questions covering the 12 major topics of the OCPJP exam.

Need help? Have questions or comments? I'd love to hear your thoughts. Email me at esteban@javapracticequestions.com.

Thanks for buying and reading this book.

Good luck on your exam,

Esteban Herrera